Building Blocks for Emergent Readers

Reading Practice Through Thematic Activities

(Fall and Winter)

Roberta Buck

Illustrated by Kathryn Marlin

Rigby Best Teachers Press ®

An imprint of Rigby ®

Dedication:
This book is dedicated to my grandmother, Roberta Gill, and our favorite story book friends, the Rag Doll and the Broomhandle.

For more information about other books from Rigby Best Teachers Press, please contact Rigby at 800-822-8661 or visit **www.rigby.com**

Editor: Mary Susnis
Executive Editor: Georgine Cooper
Designer: Biner Design
Design Production Manager: Tom Sjoerdsma
Interior Illustrations: Katheryn Marlin
Cover Illustrator: Bron Smith
Photo Credits: Cover Image © 100/Corbis, interior photos © PhotoDisc

Building Blocks for Emergent Readers
Fall and Winter

Introduction

Theme Components

Building Blocks for Emergent Readers is a valuable resource for literacy instruction using a thematic approach. It can be used as a supplement to your existing reading program or as a primary source. Because readers need to feel successful, especially in the initial stages of reading development, the thematic units in this book are designed to help children to feel confident in their abilities and to encourage them to make approximations that will set them on the path to independence.

Read the Introduction completely as there are several references to information contained here. The introduction provides a thorough description of each component of the theme, including Whole Group Reading Strategies and classroom organization and planning ideas.

Scope and Sequence

A Scope and Sequence chart is provided at the beginning of each unit. This allows you to easily identify the targeted skills for each activity. This tool provides valuable instructional information at a glance and makes it easy to see how the skills in each activity relate to your state and/or district standards.

Weekly Planner

The Weekly Planner shows you how each theme activity can be incorporated across the curriculum. It will also help you to visualize how each of these activities can be incorporated into your weekly lesson plans.

Little Books

Follow these easy directions to make a class set of the Little Books.

1. Remove the Little Book pages and copy each page twice.

2. Cut and paste the copied pages, so that you see the same text twice on one full page. For example, after copying the cover twice, cut each in half and glue both cover pages to one full 8½" x 11" sheet of paper.

3. After cutting and pasting all the pages, make a master copy of the Little Book.

4. Place the master copy on the top feeder of the photocopier.

5. The master copy will create two books, so divide the total number of copies needed in half. (For a class of twenty-four students, you will need to make twelve copies.)

    IMPORTANT: Make sure the photocopier is programmed to collate. This will automatically sort the Little Books for you.

6. Staple each booklet once at the top left corner and once about three-fourths of the page down.

7. Using a paper cutter, cut the books in half.

Introduction

Theme Components

Beginning the Theme

At the beginning of each theme, you will find a parent letter that introduces the upcoming theme. Send home a copy with every child in your class. If you plan to invite parents to participate in the activities associated with this theme, attach a personal invitation notifying parents of the opportunity for their involvement.

Let parents know in advance, perhaps during open house, that occasionally their child will be bringing home a letter requesting supplies for a special activity. A good rule of thumb is to limit requests to items totaling no more than three dollars. You can use the Supply Request Letterhead provided on page 11 to hand write a personal note to each parent from which you are requesting supplies. Ask parents to send in the items requested by a certain date. On page 8 is a Student Materials Record to help you to keep track of which students have contributed materials. Rotate through your class list to ensure that all children and parents have an opportunity to contribute.

Big Book Introduction

You will notice each theme begins with a Big Book Introduction and Whole Group Reading Strategies. The Whole Group Reading Strategies are most effective when modeled using the Big Book. You will need to create Big Books that are easily seen by all students. The Big Books are just as easy to make as the Little Books, and if you laminate them, they will last for several years.

1. Enlarge each page of the Little Book to fit on legal size paper.

2. Color the pictures.

3. Affix the book page to a large sheet of construction paper.

4. Laminate both for durability and for use with a wet-erase marker.

5. Three-hole punch, lace, or ring-bind the pages together.

The first two themes have the Day One introduction outlined page by page. The remaining themes have questions for discussion. Use the first two themes as a model as you modify the Day One lesson to meet the needs of your students.

Extension Activities

The extension activities are interdisciplinary activities including poetry, music and movement, art, cooking, math, science, and social studies. The materials that you will need for these activities can be found at the beginning of each lesson.

Caution: Some lessons include edible items. Always check for food sensitivities and allergies before serving food or allowing children to handle food.

Literature Connections

A list of trade titles can be found at the end of each theme to provide support for the weekly lessons. Some of the titles are incorporated into the extension activities, and others can be used as read alouds.

Assessment Tools

Use these blackline master assessment tools to gauge learning in the following areas: letter and number recognition, high-frequency word recognition, and vocabulary recognition.

Introduction

Theme Components

Whole Group Reading Strategies

Day Two: Revisiting the Story

Gather the children in front of you and the Big Book you have created. Show the front cover of the book and ask if anyone can remember the title of the book. Then ask children to share what happened in the story. If the story was told in a series of events, be sure to ask guiding questions like, *What was the first thing that happened, the next thing? What was the problem in the story,* and *how did it end?* Have students make connections such as:

- **Text-to-self:** *Did this story remind you of something similar that you have experienced?*

- **Text-to-text:** *Did this story remind you of something similar that you read in another book?*

- **Text-to-world:** *Can you connect the story to something in the world?*

Tell children that you are going to read the story to them. They can listen while you read, and they can read along if they choose to. Providing this stress-free opportunity allows students to make approximations with the text in a comfortable setting. You will be amazed at the number of students that read along with you!

Day Three: Echo Reading

Echo reading allows the children to hear the words correctly and follow the pitch and intonation of the reader. During echo reading, the teacher reads one sentence, and the children repeat what was read, trying to imitate the pitch and intonation. This strategy helps students read with fluency and attend to punctuation cues. As you are reading and when the children echo, follow along with your finger or a pointer.

Day Four: Choral Reading

The children will be very familiar with the story by Day Four, and most will want to read it with you. During choral reading, the children read the story aloud, together. Choral reading results in less anxiety and greater interest and enjoyment for the individual reader, and it helps to increase fluency and build sight vocabulary.

Day Five: Partner Reading

By Day Five children's Little Books are well worn with all of the reading and extension activities they have done this week. Use the partner sticks to match children up or pair them as you see fit. Have them read the story to their partner. As they are reading, walk around the room and take anecdotal notes, or use the concepts about print checklist on page 184. You may want to note left-to-right progression, return sweeps, one-to-one correspondence, high-frequency word recognition, and the use of picture cues to decipher unknown words.

Vocabulary

Introduce vocabulary words through your discussions about the book and theme. Try to provide tangible examples or hands on activities that illustrate the meaning of each word. Vocabulary word cards can be found on pages 180-183. Use the word cards to reinforce vocabulary words.

Introduction

Helpful Tools and Strategies

Framing

Framing is a term that will be used frequently during Whole Group Reading Strategies. A frame allows children to find a letter, word, sound, and so on. You will find a series of framing questions on page 10. You may want to laminate this list and keep it near your Big Book stand. You can use different frames for different questions. A larger frame might be used to find words; the smaller frame could be used to find letters or punctuation. To make the frames, use the template on page 9 and follow these directions.

1. Trace or photocopy the template onto heavy cardstock. Cut out the "finder."

2. Laminate the frame. This will create the film with which to "frame" the letter or word.

3. Cut ONLY around the outside of the frame. Leave the film over the "finder."

In addition to frames, you can also use colored transparency film to frame words and letters. Cut the film to the desired size and use a glue stick to run a line of resealable glue on one side.

Partner Sticks

Partner sticks are a unique way to match up your students so they don't always choose the same partner(s).

1. Using a marker, write lowercase letters on the top of a tongue depressors. Do the same with uppercase letters.

2. If you have twenty-four students, choose twelve lowercase letters and the matching twelve uppercase letters.

3. Hand each child one stick.

4. Once everyone has a stick, children can match lowercase and uppercase letters to find their partner.

If you have an odd number, make an extra uppercase letter. Use the letter that begins your last name so you remember which letter has a set of three. This group of three will account for the odd number of students.

To avoid pairing children who do not work well together, distribute the lowercase letters and remember the letters of particular students. When you pass out the uppercase letters, you can give those uppercase letters to children that work well with those students.

Student Materials Record

Student Name	Event						
1.							
2.							
3.							
4.							
5.							
6.							
7.							
8.							
9.							
10.							
11.							
12.							
13.							
14.							
15.							
16.							
17.							
18.							
19.							
20.							
21.							
22.							
23.							
24.							
25.							

Framing Templates

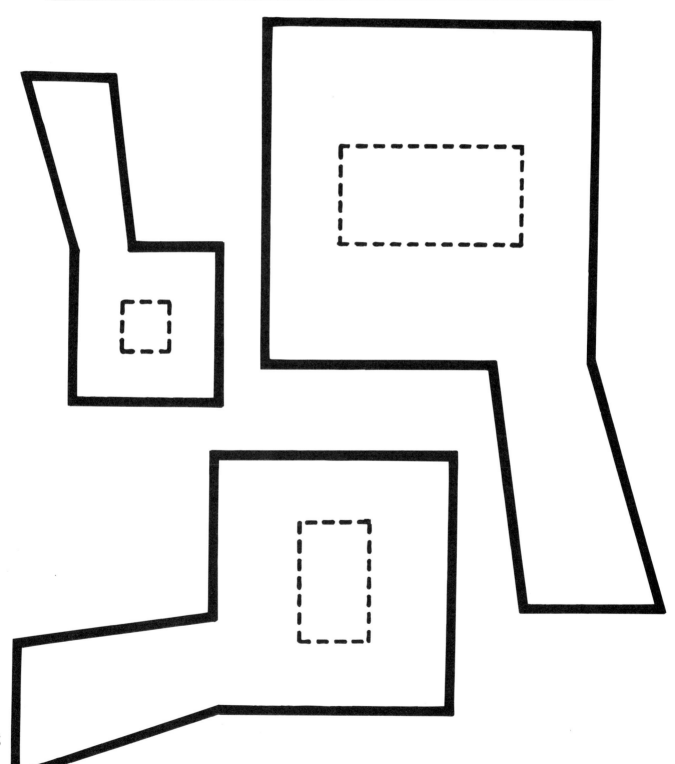

Framing Questions

Can you frame an uppercase letter?

Can you frame a lowercase letter?

Can you frame the first letter in the sentence?

Can you frame the last letter in the sentence?

Can you frame the first word in the sentence?

Can you frame the last word in the sentence?

Can you frame the letter at the beginning of your first name?

Can you frame the letter at the beginning of your last name?

Can you frame the word _____ ?

Can you frame an exclamation point?

Can you frame a period?

Can you frame a comma?

Can you frame a question mark?

Can you frame a word that rhymes with _____ ?

Supply Request

Friends and Me

Scope and Sequence

	Sound Identification	Letter Identification	Word Study (high frequency words)	Sequencing	Speaking Skills	Listening Skills	Logical Thinking Skills	Social/ Emotional Development	Large Motor Development	Fine Motor Movement
Big Book Introduction					●	●	●	●		
Revisiting				●	●	●	●	●		
Echo Reading	●	●			●	●				
Choral Reading	●	●			●	●				
Partner Reading	●	●			●	●		●		
Poem: "Me"	●	●		●	●	●		●	●	
Poem: "A Friend of Mine"					●	●	●	●		
Song: "I've Got Friends"	●			●	●	●		●		
Song: "Head, Shoulders, Knees, and Toes"				●	●	●		●	●	
Song: "We Use Five Senses"				●	●	●				●
Three-legged Race						●		●	●	
Self-Portrait						●	●	●		●
Friendship Salad					●	●	●	●		
Friendship Chart							●			
Friendship Bracelet						●	●	●		●
Friendship Salad Categories				●		●	●			
Who Is It?					●	●	●	●		
Me Bag					●	●	●	●		
Very Special Me					●	●		●		

Weekly Planner

Skills Practice: The Letter Ff	**Big Book/ Little Books** Pages 18–19	**Poetry/ Skills** Page 20	**Music and Movement** Page 21	**Art/Cooking** Page 22	**Math** Page 23	**Science** Page 24	**Social Studies** Page 24
Monday	Big Book Introduction: *Friends*		Song: "I've Got Friends"	Self Portrait	Friendship Chart		
Tuesday	Revisiting: *Friends*	Poem: "Me"	Song: "Head, Shoulders, Knees, and Toes"				Me Bag
Wednesday	Echo Reading: *Friends*	Little Book: *Friends,* the letter *Ff*	Movement: Three-legged Race		Friendship Bracelet		
Thursday	Choral Reading: *Friends*	Poem: "A Friend of Mine," the letter *Ff*	Song: "We Use Five Senses"			Who Is It? (sense of hearing)	
Friday	Partner Reading: *Friends*		Song: "I've Got Friends"	Friendship Salad	Friendship Salad Categories		Very Special Me

Friends

Name: _____

Friends play.

1

Friends share.

2

Friends laugh.

3

Friends care.

4

I have friends everywhere.

5

Date: _____

Dear Parents,

The beginning of the year brings new friendships that can last a lifetime. Next week we will be talking about the value of friends and how to be a good friend. As part of our friendship theme next week, we will be sharing our interests and what we like to do outside of school using Me Bags. Have your child decorate the outside of a brown paper lunch bag. Help your child put items inside the bag that will tell us about him or her. You may want to include a picture of your family, a baseball card (if he or she is a collector), a seashell from a favorite vacation, and so on. Please have your child bring their bag to school on _____, as we will be sharing them with our friends on that day.

During the week, we will also be celebrating new friendships by making Friendship Salad. On _____, please send a small plastic bag containing your child's choice of fruit. If it is a fruit that browns over time, leave the skin on, and I will cut it up when we are ready to use it. We will sort the fruit by kind and determine which type of fruit we have the most and least of. Finally, we will combine all the different fruits into one giant bowl and share in a tasty treat of Friendship Salad. Please alert me to any food allergies your child may have.

Thank you for your cooperation. We are off to a great start!

● Beginning the Theme

Use the Supply Request Letterhead provided on page 11 to hand write a supply request letter. You will want to send supply letters home at least one week before you plan to teach the theme. This will give parents time to send in any materials needed. Please remember to use the Student Materials Record to check off which students brought materials for this theme.

This theme requires the following supplies. Ask parents to help supply:

- bags of colored barrel beads
- paper cups and plates
- plastic spoons

Big Book Introduction

● Day One

Prereading

Introduce the Big Book, *Friends,* by creating a web. In the middle of the web write the word, *Friends.* On each of the four branches write the questions: *Who are our friends? What do friends do? Where do we make friends? Why do we make friends?* Through the creation and discussion of the web, you are activating students background knowledge and establishing a purpose for reading.

During Reading

The following lesson plan is for the first reading of *Friends.* Follow this or add your own comments and discussion questions.

Front Cover

When you introduce the Big Book to children, show the front cover and read the title. Run your finger under the title as you read. Revisit what you and the children shared in creating the web. Ask some prereading questions to get them thinking about the story and making predictions.

> *What do you think these friends will be doing in the book?*
>
> *Do you think they will be doing the same things you and your friends do?*

Page 1

Open the book to the first page. Ask children to tell you what the kids in the picture are doing. Remind them to listen carefully as you read. Be sure to point to each word as you read it. Point out how the picture matches the text.

Page 2

As you turn to the next page, ask what the kids in this picture are doing. Read the text and ask children why sharing is an important part of being a good friend.

Page 3

On the following page, make a text-to-self connection by asking children if they laugh with their friends like the kids in this picture are laughing. Read the text and check predictions made at the beginning of the reading.

Page 4

After reading this page, reinforce how it appears the friends in the picture care for each other. You might encourage your students to give the friend sitting closest to them a compliment, a pat on the back, or a handshake. Have them share other ways they can show friends they care.

Page 5

As you turn to the last page, comment on the number of pictures you see. Ask children what all of these pictures have in common. Read the text and reinforce their answers.

Post Reading

Be sure to read the story again without stopping or asking questions. Invite children to read along with you if they want. Continue pointing to the words as you read.

For the remaining day follow the Whole Group Reading Strategies.

Whole Group Reading Strategies

● Day Two
Revisiting: Friends

Have children share what they remember from the story. Help them to make a text-to-self connection by asking, *Do you and your friends do the same things that you read about yesterday?* Ask them to recall how to be a good friend. Tell children that you are going to read the story to them. They can listen as you read, and they can read it along with you.

● Day Three
Echo Reading: Friends

Pass out copies of the Little Book, *Friends,* to the class. Have children follow along in their Little Books as they echo you. Encourage them to use their fingers to match the written words to the spoken words. After reading, frame the letter *Ff* on the Big Book and have children point to it in their Little Books. Invite the children to echo you as you say the letter and the sound. Encourage them to think of words that begin with the letter *Ff*. Write the words on chart paper. Be sure to use two colored markers; one for the beginning letter, another for the remaining letters.

After reading, have children return to their seats and give them a few minutes to write their names on their Little Books and color the pictures. Invite them to use their favorite color to find and circle the letter *F* on the front cover. Follow the same procedure for the remaining pages. Collect the books for Days Four and Five.

● Day Four
Choral Reading: Friends

Distribute Little Books and read aloud together. Encourage children to point to each word as they read it. Watch for left-to-right progression and one-to-one correspondence. Collect books for Day Five.

● Day Five
Partner Reading: Friends

As children read with a partner, use the checklist on page 184 or make anecdotal notes about individual concepts about print skills. See Marie Clay's *An Observation Survey of Early Literacy Achievement* for a complete listing of print skills.

Key Vocabulary

Introduce these words throughout the week. Engage children in discussions about the words. When appropriate, provide tangible examples to illustrate the meaning of each word. Use the vocabulary word cards found on page 180 to reinforce the words.

play	laugh
share	care
special	friendship

Poetry

Print these poems on chart paper and laminate them for use with a wet erase marker. For this theme, focus on the letter *Ff*. Have volunteers find the letter in the poem and circle it. If you are using chart paper, have volunteers frame the letter *Ff*.

Have children point to their body parts as you read the following poem aloud.

 After finding the focus letter, follow with the song, "Head, Shoulders, Knees, and Toes" found on page 21.

 For this activity, use the picture cards you created in the **Friendship Chart** activity on page 23.

Choose a picture card and using tape, place it picture-side up on the blank line. After children say their friend's name aloud, turn it over and read the poem inserting the child's name.

Me

I have ten tiny fingers
And ten tiny toes,
Two tiny arms,
And one tiny nose.
One tiny mouth,
And two tiny ears,
Two tiny eyes
For smiles and tears.
One tiny head
And two tiny feet
One tiny chin—
That's me!
I'm complete.

A Friend of Mine

I have a friend
Whose name is _____,
And for hours, we will play.
We jump and run
And just have fun
At any time of day.

Music and Movement

I've Got Friends

*(Sung to the tune of
"I've Been Workin' On the Railroad")*

I've got friends to laugh and play with,
At home and at school.
I've got friends to share my toys with.
Taking turns is the rule.
Friends who care about my feelings
And know right from wrong
These are friends I like to play with
All day long!

Head, Shoulders, Knees, and Toes

Head and shoulders, knees and toes
Knees, and toes.
Head and shoulders, knees and toes
Knees, and toes.
Eyes and ears, and mouth, and nose,
Head and shoulders, knees, and toes,
Knees, and toes.

Continue to speed up the pace of the song with each recitation.

We Use Five Senses

(Sung to the tune of "Bingo")

We use five senses when we play,
 each and everyday,
See, smell, hear, taste, touch.
See, smell, hear, taste, touch.
See, smell, hear, taste, touch.
We use these when we play!

● Three-legged Race

Materials: jump ropes, pylons

You will need to watch the weather to plan for this activity. When the weather is right, borrow six jump ropes from the physical education teacher. Take the children outside and divide them into two groups. Show the children how to work together with a friend to run in a three-legged race. Demonstrate how to tie their legs together. Instruct them to run to the pylon and then return to their group. The first team to have used all their runners is the winner!

Teacher Tip: Tie the legs of the first three pairs of runners ahead of time to give yourself a head start!

Art/Cooking

● Self Portrait

Materials: 12"x18" white construction paper, crayons, markers, glue, colored construction paper

Ask children to sit in a circle and model for them how to draw a self-portrait. As you draw, be sure to talk through some of the things they will need to consider as they create their portraits—number and color of eyes, if hair is curly or straight, two hands, and two legs, and so on. You may want to even draw the clothing you are wearing.

Explain to children that they will be drawing their own portraits. As each child finishes, write his or her name in marker on the front of the portrait.

To add extra flare, bubble-cut each portrait and affix to colored construction paper. Bubble cut again, following the original form. Then hang the portraits around the classroom for a very special view!

● Friendship Salad

Always check for food sensitivities and allergies before serving food to children.

Complete the **Categories** math activity on page 23 before making your Friendship Salad.

Materials: 1 baggie of fruit from each child (See parent letter on page 17), 5 oz. paper cups, plastic spoons, large mixing bowl, large serving spoon, cutting board, and plastic knife

Allow each child to add their baggie of fruit to the bowl. Some fruit may need to be peeled and/or sliced before adding to the Friendship Salad. Be sure to have a plastic knife on hand just in case. When all students have added their fruit, give the mixture as many stirs as there are children in the class. Spoon a "healthy" serving into each cup and enjoy!

Math

● Friendship Chart

Materials: camera, film, small notecards, pocket chart, glue, marker, sentence strips

This activity is one that will last beyond the theme. Take a picture of each child and affix it to a small notecard. Be sure the notecards fit into the pockets of your pocket chart. On the back of the picture card, write the child's first name. Hang the pocket chart in a place where children have easy access to it. On the top of the pocket chart, use a sentence strip and write the question, *Which of our friends is here today?* Display the picture cards in the pocket chart with the names showing. Instruct students that when they come to school, they are to find their name card and turn it over so their picture is showing. This will teach them name recognition and help you take attendance with a quick glance. As part of your calendar routine, have children count how many friends are at school and how many are absent.

 Use with the activity and poem "A Friend of Mine" on page 20.

● Friendship Bracelet

Materials: interlocking cubes, yarn, multi-colored, plastic barrel beads (included in your supply request letter), tape, small containers

Patterning helps children learn number patterns (odd/even, counting by twos, fives, and tens). Using colored interlocking cubes, model for children how to make an *ab* pattern (i.e. red, yellow, red, yellow). Then show children how to make a friendship bracelet using the barrel beads and an *ab* pattern.

Plan this activity for small groups. Pour the barrel beads into small containers according to color. Tape one end of a six-to-eight-inch piece of yarn to the table. Have children string ten or twelve beads onto the string in an *ab* pattern. Check students' work by having them point to each bead and say the colored pattern aloud. Carefully remove the tape and tie the bracelet to their wrist clipping off excess yarn. Be sure to make the bracelets large enough so children can remove them and trade with their friends!

● Friendship Salad Categories

 Follow up with the **Friendship Salad** activity on page 22.

On the day you plan to make Friendship Salad have children sit in a circle with their baggie of fruit. Sort the fruit by type. Then create a floor graph and count the number of baggies containing each type of fruit. On chart paper, write which fruit the class had the most of (least of). Note if there are any categories with equal amounts.

Science•Social Studies

Science

● Who is it?

Materials: cards with the names of the children, a hat or bag

This interactive game teaches children about their sense of hearing.

To help build background knowledge, sing "We Use Five Senses" found on page 21.

Before you begin playing, put all children's names in a hat or bag. (Or use the Friendship Chart cards you created!) Pull one child's name from the hat. That child will be the "guesser" and will sit in a chair facing away from the class. Then select one child from the class to stand behind the guesser and say, "You're a good friend, (child's name)." The guesser responds with, "You're a good friend, too,(child's name)," filling in the name of the child he or she thinks is talking. The guesser has three chances to guess which friend is talking. Repeat until all children have a chance to be the guesser.

Social Studies

● Me Bag

Materials: brown lunch bags decorated at home

The majority of this activity should be completed at home. You will find the parent note that describes the activity on page 17. Check to make sure every child has brought a Me Bag on the day you intend to have them share their bags with the class. This activity works best when children are sitting in a circle. To keep restless hands away from rustling bags, children should keep their bags behind them until it's their turn to share.

Have additional bags on hand and allow children who may have forgotten their bag to decorate a new one. On strips of paper, write things they like to do or special memories they have and put the strips into the bag. Help them read their notes when it is their turn to share.

● Very Special Me

Materials: small mirror (compact size), box with a lid, tape or glue, wrapping paper

You will need to prepare the Very Special Me box ahead of time. Decorate the lid and the box with wrapping paper. Affix the mirror to the inside of the box.

When you are ready for the activity, have children sit in a circle. Show them the box and tell them, *There is something very special inside. It is something very unique. There is only one of its kind. It is very special to me. I think it is the most wonderful thing in the world. Are you ready to see what is inside?*

Tell children that after they look in the box, they must not share what they see. Give each child a chance to see what is so very special. Remove the lid so the mirror is visible and invite children one at a time to see what is so very special. Ask them if they can see what is special and remind them not to share what they see. Once all children have had a turn, ask them to tell you what is so special, and they will gladly shout, "Me!"

Literature Connection

Bottner, Barbara. **Two Messy Friends.** Jefferson City, MO: Cartwheel Books, 1999.

Carlson, Nancy. **My Best Friend Moved Away.** New York, NY: Viking Children's Books, 2001.

Champion, Joyce and Sucie Stevenson. **Emily and Alice Stick Together.** Orlando, FL: Harcourt, 2001.

Danzinger, Paula and Tony Ross. **It's Just in Time, Amber Brown.** New York, NY: Putnam, 2001.

Hall, Kristen. **Princess Daisy Finds a Friend.** San Francisco, CA: Chronicle Books, 1999.

Jussim, Daniel. **Double Take.** New York, NY: Viking, 2001.

Kaminsky, Jeff. **Poppy and Ella: 3 Stories About 2 Friends.** New York, NY: Hyperion Press, 2000.

Monson, A.M. and Lyn Munsinger. **Wanted: Best Friend.** Bergenfield, NJ: Dial Books for Young Readers, 1997.

Polacco, Patricia. **Betty Doll.** London, England: Philomel, 2001.

Rosenberg, Liz (Editor). **Roots & Flowers.** New York, NY: Holt, 2001.

Vainio, Pirkko and J. Alison James (Translator). **The Best of Friends.** New York, NY: North South Books, 2000.

Viorst, Judith and Robin Preiss Glasser. **Super-Completely and Totally the Messiest.** Riverside, NJ: Atheneum, 2001.

Wagner, Karen and Janet Pederson. **A Friend Like Ed.** New York, NY: Walker and Co., 1998.

Williams, Vera B. **Amber Was Brave, Essie Was Smart.** New York, NY: Greenwillow, 2001.

Zolotow, John and Amanda Harvey. **My Friend John.** Westminister, MD: Doubleday, 2000.

Colors and Shapes

Scope and Sequence

	Sound Identification	Letter Identification	Word Study (high frequency words)	Sequencing	Speaking Skills	Listening Skills	Logical Thinking Skills	Social / Emotional Development	Large Motor Development	Fine Motor Movement
Big Book Introduction	●	●	●		●	●	●			
Revisiting	●	●	●		●	●	●			
Echo Reading	●	●	●		●	●	●			●
Choral Reading	●	●	●		●	●	●			
Partner Reading	●	●	●		●	●	●	●		
Poem: "My House"	●	●	●		●	●	●			●
Poem: "Color Chant"					●	●	●	●	●	
Song: "Shapes I See"					●	●	●		●	
Walk the Shape							●		●	
Parade of Colors					●	●		●	●	
Color Wheel Chant					●	●	●			●
Shapes Bus				●	●	●	●			●
Parade of Colors Hat				●		●	●			●
Color Snack				●		●	●			
Mystery Box					●	●	●			●
Positional Terms						●	●		●	
People Graph					●	●	●	●	●	●
Techni-color Science						●	●			
Mixing Colors					●	●	●			
I Spy					●	●	●	●		

Weekly Planner

Skills Practice: The Letter *Ii* The word *I*	Big Book/ Little Books Pages 33–35	Poetry/ Skills Pages 36–38	Music and Movement Page 39–40	Art/Cooking Page 41–43	Math Page 44–45	Science Page 46	Social Studies Page 46
Monday	Big Book Introduction: *I Can See*	Poem: "My House"	Song: "Shapes I See"	Shapes Bus			I Spy
Tuesday	Revisiting: *I Can See*	Poem: "Color Chant"	Walk the Shape		Positional Terms	Mixing Colors	
Wednesday	Echo Reading: *I Can See*	Little Book: *I Can See,* the letter *Ii* and the word *I*	Song: "Color Chant"	Parade of Colors Hats and Spinner		Techni-color Science	
Thursday	Choral Reading: *I Can See*	Poem: "Color Chant"	Song: "Color Chant," or "Shapes I See"		Mystery Box		
Friday	Partner Reading: *I Can See*		Parade of Colors Color Wheel Chant	Color Snack	People Graph		

I Can See

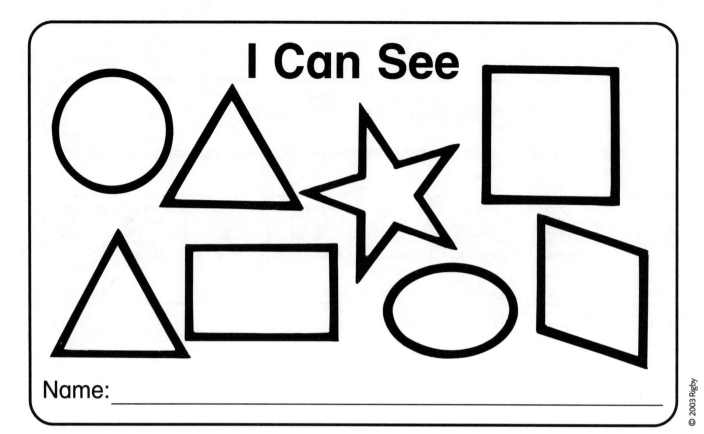

Name: _____

I can see a black cat.

1

Rigby Best Teachers Press

I can see a yellow sun.

2

I can see a red fire truck.

3

I can see a green frog.

4

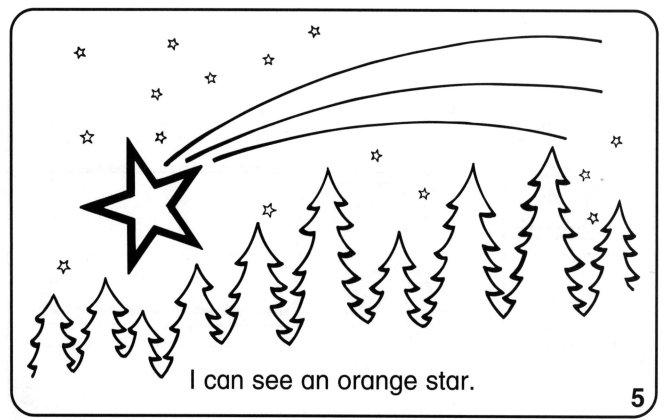

I can see an orange star.

5

I can see a brown sand castle.

6

I can see a blue kite.

7

Date _____

Dear Parents,

Next week we will be studying colors and shapes. Colors and shapes fill our world and stimulate our senses everyday. We will be discussing colors and shapes and their importance in our world. We will also learn the names and characteristics of colors and shapes. You can help reinforce these concepts with your child by pointing out colors and shapes in your everyday life. Ask your child to share the poems and/or songs that he or she is learning in school.

As a culminating activity for this unit, we will be walking in a Parade of Colors throughout the school. Please have your child wear his or her favorite solid color shirt for this activity on _____. We will create a people graph based on the different colors represented. To celebrate the end of the theme, we will eat color and shape related snacks. Please alert me to any food allergies your child may have.

       Thanks for your cooperation,

© 2003 Rigby

● Beginning the Theme

Use the Supply Request Letterhead provided on page 11 to hand write a supply request letter. You will want to send supply letters home at least one week before you plan to teach the theme. This will give parents time to send in any materials needed. Please remember to use the Student Materials Record to check off which children brought materials for this theme.

This theme requires the following supplies. Ask parents to help supply:

- **3 unused kitchen sponges**
- **Individual snack cups of cherry, lemon, and blueberry gelatin**
- **bags/boxes of colored craft sticks**

(You will need one snack cup and one craft stick per student.)

© 2003 Rigby

Big Book Introduction

● Day One

Prereading

Before reading *I Can See,* play the colors and shapes version of *I Spy*. For example, *I spy with my little eye a brown rectangle*. This rectangle could be the door to the classroom. If you feel the children are able, allow them to give clues for their classmates to discover.

During Reading

The following lesson plan is for the first reading of *I Can See*. Follow this or add your own comments and discussion questions.

Front Cover

Introduce the Big Book by showing the front cover and reading the title. Note the shapes on the cover and ask children if they found those same shapes in the classroom while playing *I Spy*. Ask prereading questions to get them thinking about the story and making predictions.

After hearing the title, do you think the story will be similar to the game we just played?

What shapes do you recognize on the front cover?

Point out the high-frequency word *I* using either a frame or colored transparency film. Tell students that this letter is special because when it is all by itself, it is the word *I* as in "*I* like to read." When it is mixed in with other letters, it helps to make other words.

Page 1

Open the Big Book to the first page. Ask children what they see. *What color is the cat? What shape is its ears? How many ears does it have?* Remind children to listen carefully as you read. Point to the words as you read them. Point out how the picture matches the text. Stress the high-frequency word *I*.

Page 2

Ask children what they see on this page. *What shape is the sun? What color is the sun? Listen as I read this page to you.* Stress the high-frequency word *I*.

Page 3

I can see something very noisy on this page. What can you see? What shape can you see in the fire truck? What color is the fire truck? Are all fire trucks red? Why do you think so? What do Mom or Dad need to do if they are in the car and they hear a fire truck coming? Why? Encourage children to follow along as you read to them. Stress the high-frequency word *I*.

Page 4

I am sure you all know what this is! Can you make the sound a frog makes? What color is this frog? Are all frogs green? How do you know that? What other color frogs have you seen? What shape is the frog's body? Follow along as I read to you. Stress the high-frequency word *I*.

Big Book Introduction

Page 5

What can you see on this page? What color is it? This shape reminds me of a song. What song do you think it reminds me of? ("Twinkle, Twinkle, Little Star.") Listen as I read to you? Stress the high-frequency word I.

Page 6

How many of you have been to the beach before? How many of you have played in a sandbox before? Have you ever built one of these? Do you recognize a shape in the sand castle? What color is the sand castle? Follow along as I read to you. Stress the high-frequency word I.

Page 7

This kite is flying high in the sky? What shape is this kite? What color is this kite? Have you ever flown a kite? Did your kite look like this? Have you ever seen a kite with a different shape? Listen as I read to you. Stress the high-frequency word I.

Post Reading

Ask children if they saw the shapes they were thinking about at the beginning of the story. Be sure to read the story again without stopping or asking questions. Invite children to read along with you if they choose. Continue pointing to the words as you read.

For the remaining days follow the Whole Group Reading Strategies.

Whole Group Reading Strategies

● Day Two
Revisiting: I Can See

Have children share what they remember from the previous day's reading. Encourage them to make a text-to-world connection by naming the shapes from the book and other places that they have seen those shapes.

 You might choose to share the song, "Shapes I See," on page 39 as an introduction to Day Two reading.

Revisit the high-frequency word *I*. Have frames or colored transparency film ready to cover the word as you read. Tell children that you are going to read the story to them. They can listen as you read and read along with you. Invite volunteers to frame or highlight the high-frequency word *I*.

● Day Three
Echo Reading: I Can See

Have children follow along in their Little Books as they echo you. Encourage them to use a colored craft stick as a pointer to match the written word to the spoken word. After reading, frame the word *I*. Stress that alone, it is a word. Invite children to find it as a letter in another word. Use the Big Book as a model.

Ask children to return to their seats and write their name on the front cover. Tell them to listen carefully as you read and color the book together. Before turning the page, ask children to recall what picture was on the first page. Instruct children to find a black crayon and color the cat black. Then instruct them to use a pencil and circle the shapes

they see. Together, name the shape. Follow the same format for the remaining pages, asking children to recall the next picture, its color, and its shape. Collect the books for the following day.

● Day Four
Choral Reading: I Can See

Distribute the Little Books and read aloud together. Encourage children to point to each word as they read it. Observe students and make anecdotal notes about left to right progression and one-to-one correspondence. Collect the books for Day Five.

● Day Five
Partner Reading: I Can See

As children read together, use the checklist on page 184 or make anecdotal notes about students' concepts about print skills. See Marie Clay's *An Observation Survey of Early Literacy Achievement* for a complete listing of print skills.

Key Vocabulary

Introduce these words throughout the week. Engage children in discussions about the words. When appropriate provide tangible examples to illustrate the meaning of each word. Use the vocabulary word cards found on page 180 to reinforce the words.

circle	blue
square	triangle
red	green

Poetry

Print these poems on chart paper. Have volunteers find the letter *Ii* and frame it or highlight it with colored transparency film.

For the following poem, use the blackline master on page 37. Have children color and cut out the shapes. Then have children manipulate the pieces to build the house as you read the poem aloud. When you are finished, ask children to glue the house scene to construction paper.

My House

My house is made of shapes; it's true.

Take a look, and I'll show you.

The windows are a perfect square,

With four sides matching,

Count the pair.

The chimney is a rectangle.

A circle forms the wreath.

The triangle-shaped tree

Makes my house complete!

For the following chant, photocopy, color and laminate the pictures on page 38. Using sticky adhesive, have children attach the pictures to the chant on the chart paper as you read aloud.

Color Chant

Colors, colors,
Oh, so bright
Follow along with all your might!
(Clap, clap, stomp–Clap, clap, stomp)

Red is an apple.
Red is a rose.
Spin around and touch your toes.
(Clap, clap, stomp–Clap, clap, stomp)

Orange is a pumpkin.
Orange is a carrot.
Echo me like you're a parrot!
(Clap, clap, stomp–Clap, clap, stomp)

Yellow is a pear.
Yellow is the sun.
Tap your head–now we're havin' fun!
(Clap, clap, stomp–Clap, clap, stomp)

Green is grass.
Green is a pea.
Wiggle all about, if you please.
(Clap, clap, stomp–Clap, clap, stomp)

Blue is the sky.
Blue is the sea.
Jump up and down, just like me.
(Clap, clap, stomp–Clap, clap, stomp)

Brown is chocolate.
Brown is sand.
Show me your fingers and wiggle your hands.
(Clap, clap, stomp–Clap, clap, stomp)

Black is licorice.
Black is night.
Thanks for chanting with all your might!
(Clap, clap, stomp–Clap, clap, stomp)

Poetry

"My House"

Poetry

Color Chant

Music and Movement

The following song can be sung along as you flip through the pages of the Big Book.

Shapes I See

(Sung to the tune of "I'm a Little Teapot")

This little black cat has pointy ears.
If you know their shape, give a great big cheer.
Draw it in the air and on the ground.
Let me hear you say it out loud.
   Children say: **Triangle**

The bright sun is so hot up in the sky.
If you know its shape, give your neighbor a high-five.
Draw it in the air and on the ground.
Let me hear you say it out loud.
   Children say: **Circle**

When you hear a fire truck, you know what to do.
If you see a rectangle with your fingers show me two.
Draw it in the air and on the ground.
Let me hear you say it out loud.
   Children say: **Rectangle**

ump and swim. That's what they do.
its body shape shout, "Yahoo!"
e air and on the ground.
ou say it out loud.
   Oval

When you see this shape, you can make a wish.
If you know its name, clap your hands like this.
   (clap two times)
Draw it in the air and on the ground.
Let me hear you say it out loud.
   Children say: **Star**

Do you see the shape hidden in the sand?
If you think you can, raise your left hand.
Draw it in the air and on the ground.
Let me hear you say it out loud.
   Children say: **Square**

Do you know the shape on the end of the string?
If yes is your answer, flap your arms like wings.
Draw it in the air and on the ground.
Let me hear you say it out loud.
   Children say: **Diamond**

Music and Movement

● Walk the Shape

Materials: colored masking tape, construction paper shapes cut from the same color as the masking tape, opaque bag

Using a different colored masking tape for each shape, create one large triangle, square, circle and rectangle on the floor. Create smaller versions using construction paper. Make at least one shape for each child in the class. Create one of each shape as a master set.

Divide the class into four groups. Distribute a shape to each child in the group, varying the shapes within each group. Review the shapes and their elements. Put the master set in an opaque bag. Explain to students that you will pull a shape from the bag. Children holding that shape will then have an opportunity to walk on the shape, as if it were a balance beam. Children who can walk on the shape without "falling off" will earn one point for their team. There will be no demerits. If they should "fall," their team will not earn a point. Use tallies to keep score.

● Parade of Colors

As a culminating activity to the theme on colors and shapes, children will wear their favorite solid colored shirt to school and march in a Parade of Colors.

 While parading in their hats and T-shirts, children can chant this color poem.

Color Wheel

See the spinner on the wheel
Who knows what it will reveal?
It may be red, yellow, or blue
Primary colors just for you.

Secondary colors are in between,
They are purple, orange, and green.
Watch the spinner and the wheel,
What color will it reveal?

Art/Cooking

● Shapes Bus

Materials: 9" x 12" construction paper in the following colors: yellow, red, blue, white, and black; glue

If you organize the materials ahead of time, this can be done as a whole group listening activity. Copy the following shapes onto heavy cardstock and cut them out. You may want to create one template per table group.

 Bus shape (approximately 7" tall and 11" wide).

 Circle (approximately 3¾" diameter) wheels

 Triangle (3¾" base, 3" height, 3½" sides)

 Rectangle (4" wide, 1¾" tall)

 Rectangle (4½" wide, 1½" tall) Children will cut it into thirds to make the windows.

In order to use the construction paper efficiently, cut the black 9" x 12" construction paper in half. Then cut the red, blue, and white 9" x 12" paper in fourths. Then cut the blue and white fourths into halves. Each student will need:

- One 9" x 12" yellow paper to trace the bus
- 1 red square to trace the triangle
- 1 half sheet of black paper for the two wheels
- 1 blue rectangle to make the square windows
- 1 white rectangle

Invite children to sit in a circle and model for them how to create the bus. Explain that after you demonstrate the project, they will go back to their tables, listen carefully to directions, and then make their own shapes bus.

Model the following directions as you create a sample shapes bus:

Trace the bus on the yellow paper and cut it out. Using a pencil, put your name on one side and turn it over. Talk about the front, back, top, and bottom of the bus. Explain to children how to tell the difference. (The front and the top are round. The back and the bottom are flat.)

 An explanation of positional terms is in the math section of this theme on page 44.

Trace two circles on the black paper and cut them out. Ask children, *Should the wheels go on the top of the bus or the bottom?* Remind them that the bottom is flat. Then glue the wheels in place.

Trace the triangle on the red paper and cut it out. Review the properties of a triangle. Ask children, *Does the triangle belong on the front side of the bus or the back?* Glue it in place.

With the blue rectangle, show children how to cut it into three squares. (You might want to have extra blue rectangles handy. Making equal thirds is tricky.) Ask children, *Do the windows belong at the top of the bus or the bottom of the bus?* Glue the windows in place.

The last shape is the rectangle. Ask children, *Does the rectangle belong in front of the triangle or behind the triangle?* Glue it in place.

When you are finished modeling how to make a shapes bus, allow children to return to their seats. When children have all their supplies, allow them trace and cut the shapes they will need. Stress that they should not glue anything yet. Monitor students as they trace and cut.

When all children have finished tracing and cutting out their shapes, direct them to assemble the bus shape by shape. Use positional terms as they build. Ask why questions such as *Why can't the wheels go on top? Why can't the windows be on the bottom?* Continue with this process until the buses are complete.

Have children clean up their scraps. You might choose to sing "Wheels on the Bus" as they clean up and put away supplies. Ask children to return to their seats to review positional terms and shapes.

● Parade of Colors Hat

Materials: 12" x 18" white construction paper, crayons, color wheel found on page 43, brads, glue, hole punch, yarn

Prepare the hats for students ahead of time. Create a hat pattern by drawing a triangle that is eight inches from base to peak and eight inches on each side. Connect the two corners of the base as shown. You might choose to have a parent volunteer trace, cut, and hole punch the hats. Then they can tie a six-inch piece of string through each hole. Give each child a hat pattern and have them put their name on one side of the hat and decorate the other side.

Using the template on page 43, photocopy a color wheel and a spinner for each student. Color the color wheel (with primary and secondary colors) and cut it out. Place the color wheel on construction paper and trace around it. Cut it out and glue the color wheel to the construction paper circle for durability. Color and cut out the spinner. Fasten the spinner to the color wheel with the brad and attach the wheel to the hat. Bring the sides of the hat together to form a cone and staple. Set the hats aside for the parade on the last day of the theme.

● Color Snack

See the **Techni-color Science** experiment on page 46.

After reading aloud the book *Mouse Paint* by Ellin Stoll Walsh complete the Techni-color Science activity on page 46. For a primary color snack, ask parents to bring in individual gelatin cups, in the following flavors: cherry (red), lemon (yellow), and blueberry (blue). You might choose to have the snack on the day of your Parade of Colors.

Art/Cooking

Color Wheel and Spinner

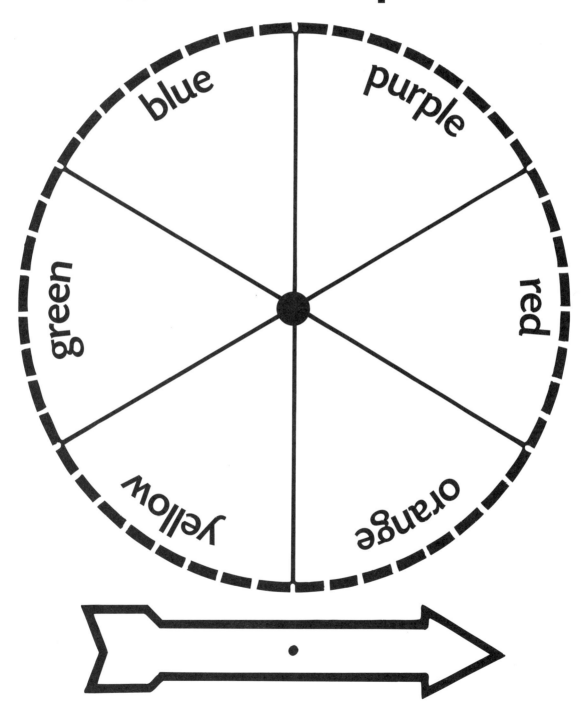

Math

● Mystery Box

Materials: kitchen sponges cut into shapes, shoebox, tape, and scissors

Using kitchen sponges, cut out the seven shapes that are used in the Little Book. Create a mystery box from an old shoebox. Tape the lid closed and decorate the box. Cut a circle in one end large enough for a child's hand to fit into.

Before the activity, dampen the sponges so they can be easily manipulated. Show the shapes and discuss the names and properties of each shape with children. Then put the shapes in the mystery box. Explain to children that when the box is passed to them, they will be given clues for a particular shape. From those clues, they will have to name the shape and using their sense of touch, put their hand into the mystery box to find the shape. You might choose to use the following clues.

Triangle–This shape has three corners and three sides.

Circle–This shape starts at the top and goes round and round.

Rectangle–This shape has two short sides and two long sides.

Oval–This shape looks like a circle, but it is wider in the middle.

Star–This shape has five points.

Square–This shape has four sides that are all the same length.

Diamond–This shape has four sides and looks like a kite.

● Positional Terms

Materials: shapes bus

 Use this activity after completing the **Shapes Bus** on pages 41–42.

To help children learn positional terms, incorporate the idea into kinesthetic and manipulative activities. Children will have engaged in a discussion around positional terms while building their shapes bus. Now direct children to manipulate the bus above their head, behind their back, beside their leg, below the table, on their lap, and near their foot. Repeat until children are successful with the movements.

● People Graph

On the last day of the theme, children will wear a T-shirt of their favorite color. (See the parent note on page 32 of this theme.) Before the Parade of Colors have children sort themselves by colors. Direct them to line up, one behind the other, creating a people bar graph. Have children rote count each group. As each group counts off, write the total number in the group on a piece of paper and have the last child hold it above their head, facing the remainder of their line. Now compare numbers. Point out the least, most, and any that are equal. Record these findings on chart paper.

Provide children with copies of the T-shirt pattern on page 45. Instruct them to color the T-shirt the same color as the shirt they are wearing and cut it out. Using their colored T-shirts, have children create a graph identical to the people graph. Instruct children to tape their T-shirts to a wall. Place the paper with the number next to the appropriate column. Review the graph to ensure that it matches the information on the chart paper.

Math

People Graph T-shirt Template

Science•Social Studies

Science

● Techni-color Science

Materials: a clear 12-ounce jar, food coloring, $\frac{1}{3}$ cup vegetable oil, salt

This experiment will show children how some liquids, when combined together, just won't mix. Fill a twelve-ounce jar with water. Add your favorite color food coloring. Add $\frac{1}{3}$ cup vegetable oil and observe the layers as they settle. Have children count to five as you shake salt into the jar. Encourage children to watch carefully as the oil and salt form a blob and sink to the bottom. Explain to children that as the salt dissolves in the water, the oil should float back to the top. Ask children what can be done to make the action repeat? (Add more salt.) Have children make predictions as to why this works.

Oil does not dissolve in water. It is lighter than water; therefore, it floats on top. Salt is heavier than water, and it will dissolve in water. When you add the salt to the oil, it drags the oil to the bottom. As the salt dissolves, it is no longer heavy enough to hold down the oil, and the oil floats back to the top.

● Mixing Colors

Materials: red, blue, and yellow food coloring, six transparent mixing bowls, spoons, turkey baster, *Mouse Paint* by Ellin Stoll Walsh

Before reading *Mouse Paint* by Ellin Stoll Walsh, prepare one small bowl of red, yellow, and blue water. Be sure the mixtures are in clear containers.

Have three additional clear containers ready for the secondary colors. Introduce the three colors to children as the primary colors—the colors from which other colors are made. Show and read the cover of the book. Ask children why the author might have titled this story *Mouse Paint*. Allow children to make predictions. Guide their thinking to have them consider what would happen if the mice found some wet paint. *What might happen if the colors mixed together?* Have them make a text-to-self connection by asking if they have ever mixed colors while they were painting. *What happened?*

As you read the story, create the new colors using the food coloring. Use a turkey baster to combine the colors. After reading the book, reinforce the idea of primary and secondary colors. Prepare a color wheel beginning with primary colors and then adding secondary colors.

 Refer to your color wheel when children create their **Parade of Colors Hats** (see page 43).

Social Studies

● I Spy

To encourage higher level thinking skills and develop student to student interaction, play the game I Spy with children. Begin by modeling the process. *I spy with my little eye a rectangle. This rectangle leads us into and out of our classroom.* (Door) When you feel children understand the concept, allow them to find the shapes and give the clues.

Literature Connection

Bennett, Madeline and Gary Bennett. ***The Silliest Shapes and Colors in the Wild West.*** Phoenix, AZ: Arizona Highways, 2001.

Brown, Margaret Wise. ***The Color Kittens.*** Westminister, MD: Golden Books, 2000.

Burke, Jennifer. ***Triangles (City Shapes).*** Danbury, CT: Children's Press, 2000.

Derolf, Shane and Michael Letzig. ***The Crayon Box That Talked.*** Westminister, MD: Random House, 1997.

Emberly, Ed. ***The Wing on a Flea.*** Boston, NY: Little Brown, 2001.

Gill, Shelley and Shannon Cartwright. ***Count Alaska's Colors.*** Homer, AK: Paws IV, 1997.

Hoban, Tana. ***Shapes, Shapes, Shapes.*** Glenview, IL: Scott Foresman, 1996.

Jonas, Ann. ***Color Dance.*** New York, NY: Greenwillow, 1989.

Kessler, Leonard. ***Mr. Pine's Purple House.*** Keller, TX: Purple House Press, 2000.

MacDonald, Suse. ***Sea Shapes.*** Madison, WI: Gulliver Books, 1994.

MacKinnon, Debbie and Anthea Sieveking. ***Eye Spy Colors.*** Watertown, MA: Charlesbridge, 1998.

Murphy, Chuck. ***Color Surprises.*** New York, NY: Little Simon, 1997.

Murphy, Stuart J. and Edward Miller. ***Circus Shapes (Mathstart).*** New York, NY: Harper Trophy, 1998.

Peek, Merle. ***Mary Wore Her Red Dress.*** Wilmington, MA: Houghton Mifflin, 1988.

Rau, Dana Meachen. ***A Star in My Orange: Looking for Nature's Shapes.*** Fresno, CA: Milbrook Press, 2002.

Thong, Roseanne and Grace Lin. ***Round is a Mooncake: A Book of Shapes.*** San Francisco, CA: Chronicle Books, 2000.

Williams, Sue and Julie Vivas. ***I Went Walking.*** Orlando, FL: Harcourt, 1992.

Apples

Scope and Sequence

	Sound Identification	Letter Identification	Word Study (high frequency words)	Sequencing	Speaking Skills	Listening Skills	Logical Thinking Skills	Social /Emotional Development	Large Motor Development	Fine Motor Movement
Big Book Introduction				●	●	●	●			
Revisiting			●	●	●	●	●			
Echo Reading	●	●	●	●	●	●	●			
Choral Reading	●	●	●	●	●	●	●			
Partner Reading	●	●	●	●	●	●	●	●		
Poem: "Apples A-plenty"	●	●			●	●	●	●	●	
Poem: "Apple Treat"	●	●			●	●				
Song: "Bushel Basket"	●				●	●				
Song: "Apple, Apple on the Tree"	●				●	●	●			
Apple Shaker Rhythms						●	●		●	
Wheelbarrow Race						●		●	●	
Apple Cereal Necklace						●	●			●
Sponge Paint Apple Trees						●				●
Apple Sandwiches						●				●
Apple Taste Test					●	●				
Apple Shakers						●				●
How Many Apples Tall?					●	●	●	●	●	
Which Is Your Favorite?					●	●	●			●
Adding One More					●	●	●			●
Which Weighs More?					●	●	●			
Parts of an Apple Poster					●	●	●			
Why Does an Apple Change Color?					●	●	●			
Sink or Float?					●	●	●			
Johnny Appleseed					●	●	●	●		

Weekly Planner

Skills Practice: The letter *Aa* The word *is*	Big Book/ Little Books Pages 54–55	Poetry/ Skills Pages 56	Music and Movement Pages 57	Art/Cooking Pages 58–61	Math Pages 62–64	Science Page 65	Social Studies Page 66
Monday	Big Book Introduction: *The Apple Tree*	Poem: "Apples A-plenty"	Song: "Bushel Basket" Wheelbarrow Race	Apple Cereal Necklace	Adding One More	Parts of an Apple Poster	
Tuesday	Revisiting: *The Apple Tree,* the word *is*		Song: "Apple, Apple on the Tree"	Sponge Paint Apple Trees	How Many Apples Tall?		
Wednesday	Echo Reading: *The Apple Tree*	Poem: "Apple Treat," Little Book: *The Apple Tree,* the letter *Aa* and the word *is*	Song: "Bushel Basket"	Apple Taste Test	Which Is Your Favorite?		
Thursday	Choral Reading: *The Apple Tree*	Little Book: *The Apple Tree,* the letter *Aa* and the word *is*	Song: "Apple, Apple on the Tree"	Apple Sandwiches	Adding One More	Why Does the Apple Change Color?	Johnny Appleseed
Friday	Partner Reading: *The Apple Tree*		Song: "Bushel Basket" Apple Shaker Rhythms	Apple Shakers	Which Weighs More?	Sink or Float?	

The Apple Tree

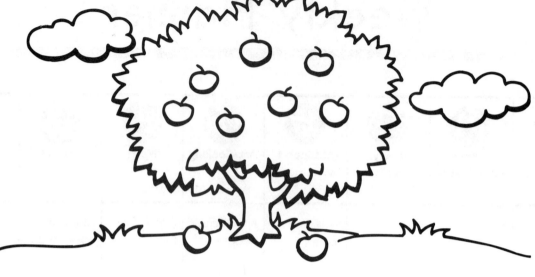

Name: _____

©　2003 Rigby

This is the apple tree in spring.

1

© 2003 Rigby

This is the apple tree in summer.

2

This is the apple tree in fall.

3

This is the apple tree in winter.

4

Which tree do you like most of all?

5

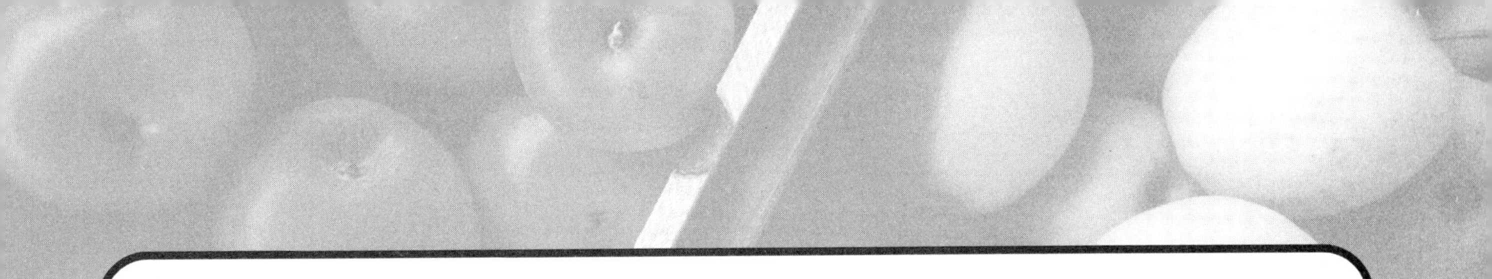

Date _____

Dear Parents,

We will begin to explore a new fall theme next week. We will delve into all the delicious aspects of one of America's favorite fruits–the apple. As a part of our studies, please have your child bring **one apple** (any kind) to school on _____.
In addition to learning how apples grow and learning the parts of an apple, we will be participating in many other fun and tasty apple activities. Please alert me to any food allergies your child may have.

You can help your child at home by reinforcing the concepts we are exploring during the school day. Have your child retell the stages of an apple tree in each season or name the parts of an apple. Invite your child to sing the songs we are learning or to recite the poems we have read.

Your effort and cooperation are truly appreciated.

    Thank you,

● Beginning the Theme

Use the Supply Request Letterhead provided on page 11 to write a supply request letter. You will want to send supply letters home the week before you plan to teach the theme. This will give parents time to send in any materials needed. Please remember to use the Student Materials Record to check off which students brought materials for this theme.

This theme requires the following supplies. Ask parents to help supply:

- 1 large jar of apple sauce
- 1 gallon of apple cider
- 1 store-bought apple pie
- 1 jar of peanut butter
- 2 boxes of apple flavored cereal (O-shaped)

Big Book Introduction

● Day One

Prereading

Because children were asked to prepare for the theme by bringing in an apple, they will be anxious to learn more about apples.

 You can introduce the theme by showing the Parts of an Apple poster (See page 65 for directions on how to create the poster).

Activate children's background knowledge by showing one of the apples and comparing it to the poster. Discuss the outside of the apple (skin, stem). Then open the poster to reveal the inside of the apple. Ask volunteers to point to and name the parts of the apple they know. *Do apples grow in the ground or on a tree? What season do we pick apples from their trees? What happens to the apple tree in the winter, spring, and summer?* Allow children to share ideas. Divide chart paper into fourths and label each box: spring, summer, fall, and winter. Beginning with fall, ask children to share what the apple tree might look like during this season. Then follow with winter, spring, and summer. Tell children to listen carefully as you read *The Apple Tree* to see if their predictions are correct.

During Reading

After reading the title, ask children what season they think this apple tree on the cover is in. Why? As you read the Big Book, use the procedures and questioning techniques presented in the previous units as a guide for sharing this book with the children. Use your finger to model one-to-one correspondence of the written word to the spoken word. Remind children to listen carefully and to refer to the chart to check their predictions as you read.

Post Reading

Go back to the first page and reread the text. Direct children to the chart and share their predictions. *Were your predictions correct? Is there anything you would like to add?* Invite a volunteer to come up to the chart and add an illustration of an apple tree in spring. Continue to do the same for the remaining seasons.

Be sure to read the story again without stopping or asking questions. Invite children to read along with you if they want. Continue pointing to the words as you read.

For the remaining days follow the Whole Group Reading Strategies.

Whole Group Reading Strategies

● Day Two
Revisiting: **The Apple Tree**

Show the seasons of the apple tree chart you created on the previous day. Ask children what they remember from the previous day's reading. Share the title of the story. Read the first page of the story and focus on the high-frequency word *is*. As you revisit the story, frame or highlight the high-frequency word. Encourage children to read along with you. Point to the word *is* and allow children to read the word by themselves. Make *The Apple Tree* Big Book available for exploration during children's free time.

● Day Three
Echo Reading: **The Apple Tree**

Distribute the Little Books to children. Have them follow along in the books as they echo you. Encourage them to use their finger to match the written words to the spoken word. After reading *The Apple Tree*, review the high-frequency word *is*. Then direct children to look at the word *apple*. Invite a volunteer to frame the first letter of the word *Aa*. *What sound do you hear at the beginning of the word apple? Can you put your finger on the letter that makes that sound?* On chart paper, brainstorm words that begin with the letter *Aa*. As you write the words, use two colors. Use one color for the beginning sound and another color for the remaining letters. If children suggest words that begin with the long /ā/ sound, explain that the letter *Aa* can make two sounds /ă/ as in *ăpple* or /ā/ as in *āte*.

After reading, give children a few minutes to write their name on the Little Book and color the pictures. Invite them to use their favorite color to

find and circle the letter *Aa* on the front cover. Follow the same procedure for the remaining pages. Collect the books for Days Four and Five.

● Day Four
Choral Reading: **The Apple Tree**

Distribute the Little Books and read aloud together. Encourage children to use their finger to point as they read. Watch for left-to-right progression and one-to-one correspondence. Focus on the word *is* and add it to your word wall. Collect books for Day Five.

● Day Five
Partner Reading: **The Apple Tree**

As children read together, use the checklist on page 184 or make anecdotal notes about children's concepts about print skills. See Marie Clay's *An Observation Survey of Early Literacy Achievement* for a complete listing of print skills.

Key Vocabulary

Introduce these words throughout the week. Engage children in discussions about the words. When appropriate provide tangible examples to illustrate the meaning of each word. Use the vocabulary word cards found on page 181 to reinforce the words.

seeds	stem	leaf
meat	core	skin

Poetry

Apples A-plenty

Apples a-plenty
Apples galore,
I can't get enough,
I always want more.
Red apples, yellow apples, green apples, too
They're juicy and crunchy
And so good for you!

Apple Treat

Applesauce, apple juice, apple pie——
I can't decide which one to try.
I bet they are sweet
And oh, what a treat!
Which one is your favorite? Why?

 Use this poem with the Taste Test activity (see page 59).

After reading this poem aloud, have children sit in a circle holding the apple they brought to school. Invite them to sort the apples by color. Then discuss each apple's classification. To classify the apples, create table tents (see illustration right) from index cards with these names:

Red Delicious (deep red in color, five buttons on the bottom, shaped like an oval and sweet)

McIntosh (reddish-green, round, and somewhat tart)

Golden Delicious (yellow in color, shaped like an oval, and usually sweet)

Granny Smith (green, round, and tart enough to make your lips pucker)

Other (Describe the characteristics of the apples that do not fall into the other categories)

Read this poem aloud emphasizing the /ă/ and /ā/ sounds as you read. After reading the poem, invite volunteers to frame or highlight all the *a*'s in the poem. If students point out the letter *a* in the words *sauce* or *treat*, briefly explain that sometimes the letter *a* works with a partner to produce a different sound. Focus on the /ă/ and /ā/ sounds.

Music and Movement

Bushel Basket
(Sung to the tune of "A Tisket, A Tasket")

A tisket, a tasket,
I've got my bushel basket.
I'll pick some apples from the tree
And share them with my family.

Apple, Apple on the Tree
(Sung to the tune of "Twinkle, Twinkle, Little Star")

Apple, apple on the tree
You will taste so good to me.
Shall I bake you in a pie?
Warm and sweet, I think I'll try.
Apple, apple on the tree,
Apple pie is so YUMMY!

Apple, apple on the tree
You will taste so good to me.
Apple juice is never sour,
I could drink it every hour.
Apple, apple on the tree
Apple juice is right for me!

Apple, apple on the tree
You will taste so good to me.
With a meal or as a snack,
Applesauce makes my lips smack.
Apple, apple on the tree
Applesauce fills me with glee!

● Apple Shaker Rhythms

 See page 59 for directions on how to make **Apple Shakers**.

Encourage children to practice shaking their apples. When everyone's apple shaker is complete, invite children to follow a shaking pattern: *shake-shake, pause, shake-shake, pause;* or *shake-shake-shake, stomp, stomp, shake-shake-shake, stomp, stomp,* and so on. Try shaking it along to one of the apples songs, too.

● Wheelbarrow Race

Materials: two pylon cones

Weather permitting, take children outside to a grassy area and divide them into two teams. Ask children to share what a wheelbarrow is and how it is used. Relate the wheelbarrow to the apple theme by pointing out that a load of apples could be easily moved from place to place in a wheelbarrow. Ask if anyone has ever participated in a wheelbarrow race before? Invite a volunteer to help you model the activity. Have a child lie on his or her stomach. Standing near the child's feet, grasp his or her ankles and lift. Have the child use his or her hands to push up his or her body weight. Ask the child to walk forward on his or her hands while you follow behind, holding up his or her legs. Have a cone or some sort of marker at the opposite end of the starting line. The teams will have to "wheel" around the cone and come back to the starting line.

Note: Check the area for stray objects before you begin the activity.

Art/Cooking

● Apple Cereal Necklace

Always check for food sensitivities and allergies before serving food to children.

Materials: red, yellow, or green yarn cut into 15" strips (enough for each child in your class), tape, plastic bowl (one for each group), apple-flavored cereal in an O-shape (Two boxes should be enough for a class of twenty and will provide leftovers for a snack.)

 Use the Adding One More activity on page 63 as an introduction to this fine motor skill activity.

Tape one end of a 15" piece of yarn to the table for each child. Place a plastic bowl full of cereal in the middle of each table. Remind children to listen carefully to directions. Invite them to thread one piece of cereal on their necklace. Revisit the concept of "one more." *If you have one piece of cereal on your necklace and you add one more, how many will you have all together?*

Count the pieces together. Remind children to touch-count each piece. Be sure to give lots of positive reinforcement. *Good job, great counting! We now have two cereal pieces on our necklace. If we add one more, how many will we have all together?* Touch-count each piece. Continue with this pattern until children have ten cereal pieces on their necklaces. Instruct children to leave the necklace taped to the table until you come around and tie it. Tell them it is taped so that the pieces do not slip off the end. While they are waiting for you, children can share the leftover cereal in the bowl by eating one piece at a time. Each time they eat a piece they can say, *One more!*

● Sponge Paint Apple Trees

Materials: 12" x 18" white construction paper, six to eight clothespins (depending on the number of children painting at one time), two to three large sponges cut into 2" x 2" squares, six to eight cork stoppers (You can find these at most craft stores.), green and red poster paint

Before painting, use a brown marker to create a tree trunk on the narrow edge of each 12" x 18" paper. Attach a clothespin to each of the sponge squares.

Model for children how to paint the apple trees. *First put your name on the back of the paper. Holding the clothespin, dip only the end of the sponge into green paint. Gently dab the sponge all over the top of the paper to create the leaves of the tree. Leave some white spaces for your round, red apples. To create the apples, hold the cork with the tips of your fingers, dip the end into the red paint and gently press it onto the paper.* Remind children to paint the red apples on the white spaces they saved. Help children place their paintings in the drying rack. When the paint is dry, write the child's name on the front of the paper. Display the pictures.

● Apple Sandwiches

Caution: Peanut product used in this activity.

Always check for food sensitivities and allergies before serving food to children.

Materials: small plastic bowls (one for each table), peanut butter (creamy), popsicle sticks, large spoon, sharp knife or apple slicer, paper towels, small paper plates

Prior to the activity, wash and dry the apples children brought to school. Provide each table with

Art/Cooking

a small bowl of peanut butter and give each child a popsicle stick to use as a spreader.

Cut an apple in half for each child. Have children remove all of the seeds and set them on a paper towel to dry. When children have finished removing the seeds from their apples, slice each apple half for them and model how to make an apple sandwich. Using the popsicle stick, spread peanut butter on one apple slice and place another slice on top. Eat and enjoy!

When children are finished eating their sandwiches have them clean up their space, taking care to save the seeds that are drying on the paper towel.

 When everyone is finished, use the seeds to complete the apple shaker activity on this page.

● Apple Taste Test

Always check for food sensitivities and allergies before serving food to children.

Materials: apple juice, apple pie, applesauce, small paper plates, small kitchen cups, plastic spoon or fork, photocopies of the apple pictures (page 60).

 You might choose to introduce this activity by choral reading the poem, "Apple Treat" or by singing the song, "Apple, Apple on the Tree" on pages 56-57.

Send a handwritten Supply Request Letter (see page 53) to ensure that you will have the items needed for this activity. Copy the patterns on page 60 so students can choose a picture to represent their favorite apple treat. Give each child a small plate with a spoonful of each: apple pie, applesauce,

and a small cup of apple juice. Together, try each of the apple items. Instruct children to decide which one is their favorite. After they have finished each of the items from their taste test, have them choose the picture that represents their favorite apple treat and color it.

 See the **Taste Test Graph** activity on page 62 to extend this activity.

● Apple Shaker

Note: To complete this activity, children will need the seeds from the Apple Sandwiches activity (see page 58).

Materials: red, brown, and green construction paper

Copy the apple templates on page 61 onto heavy card stock. Create at least two tracing patterns of each template for every table. With children sitting in a circle, model this art activity.

Trace the pieces onto the correct colored paper and cut them out. You will need two red apple shapes, one brown stem, and one green leaf. Glue the stem to the top of one of the apples. Then glue the leaf (pointing upwards) to the bottom of the stem. Finally, place a small amount of glue around the edge of the apple and place the other apple shape on top. Make sure not to glue the flaps on the side. This is where you will drop in the apple seeds. Write the children's names on the leaves and set them aside to dry. To complete the shaker, children will need the seeds from their apple sandwiches. After children have put in their apple seeds, help them fold in the slots and staple the edge closed. Instruct children to gently hold the shaker around the edges and shake, shake, shake!

Art/Cooking

Apple Taste Test

Art/Cooking

Apple Shaker Template

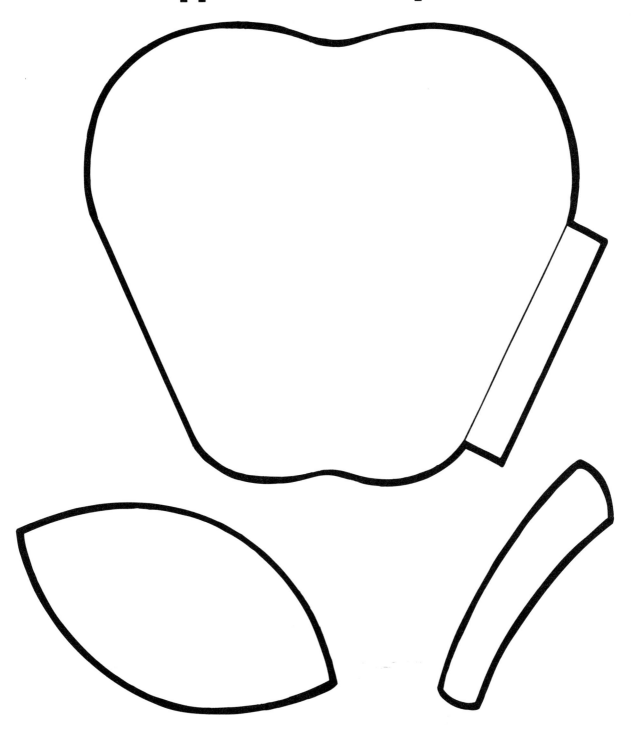

Math

● How Many Apples Tall?

Materials: small, medium, and large apple templates, construction paper

Photocopy the blackline master on page 64 three times and cut out one small apple, one medium apple, and one large apple. Trace the apple patterns on colored construction paper. For example, make the small apples red, medium apples green, and large apples yellow. Create several of each size. If you laminate the construction paper apples, they will last year after year. Have children sit in a circle. Show the three sizes of apples to children. Have them categorize each size as small, medium, or large. Invite a volunteer to lie on the floor in the middle of the circle. Hold up the medium apple. *How many apples tall do you think (child's name) is?* Allow children to share their estimates.

Model how you can measure using the apples. Starting at the child's heel, place apple on top of apple (use the medium apple), counting each until you reach the top of the child's head. Check to see if any estimates were correct. Invite children to estimate how many small apples it will take to measure the same child. Measure the child again using the small apples. *Did you need more or less small apples? Were any of our estimates correct?*

Using the partner sticks (page 7), pair off children. Give children a set of small, medium, or large apples and have them measure their partner. Remind children to first estimate the number of apples it will take to measure their partner, then measure from heel to head. Invite children to try the other apples, too. Later, put one set of each of the apples in the math center. Encourage children to measure objects around the classroom during free choice time.

● Which Is Your Favorite? (Taste Test Graph)

Materials: butcher paper, colored copy of each of the apple treats, tape, chart paper

 This activity is for use after children have participated in the **Apple Taste Test** and have chosen the picture that represents their favorite apple treat (see page 60).

Either in your classroom or in the hallway, set up a floor-to-ceiling graph. At the top of a large sheet of construction paper write the label, "Which is Your Favorite?" Color one of each of the apple patterns on page 60 and tape them at the bottom of the graph. Ask children to use the picture of their favorite apple treat (applesauce, apple juice, apple pie) and tape it above the corresponding graph piece. You will need to monitor the spacing between each picture so the graph is visually correct. When everyone has added his or her picture to the graph, analyze the results. Have children look at the graph and tell which is the most, least popular. *How can you tell? Are any the same?* Count the results for each treat. On chart paper, record the total number of votes for each treat. *Is it an odd number or an even number?* Record the numbers with tally marks. Make the graph available for children to revisit.

Math

● Adding One More

 This lesson should be done before children make their **Apple Cereal Necklaces.** (see page 58).

Invite children to sit in a circle. Give each child ten plastic interlocking cubes. Together count the cubes. Model for children how to touch and pull aside each cube as you count it. Introduce the concept of one more by building a tower. Tell children to pick up one cube. Repeat that each child has one. Tell children to add one more cube to their tower. *How many do you have in your tower now? Start at the bottom and touch each cube as you count your way up the tower.* Repeat the process until you have a tower of ten.

Model the Apple Cereal necklace activity (page 58) for children while you are still sitting in a circle.

● Which Weighs More?

Materials: a primary balance, chart paper, markers, a small apple, a variety of classroom objects such as teddy bear counters, a pair of blunt scissors, several crayons, a deck of cards, a supply of pennies

When you collect items to measure, ensure that you have one or two items that will weigh more than a small apple. Invite children to sit in front of the balance. Put the same number of pennies in each basket and show children how the sides are equal. Add more pennies to one of the baskets. *What happens? Why?* Invite a volunteer to choose a small apple from the class collection. Remove the pennies from one side of the balance and put the apple in their place. *What happens? Why?* On chart paper, create a poster similar to the one above.

Show children the objects. Encourage children to predict which will be heavier, the apple or the objects. Put the apple in one side of the balance and the objects in the other side. Observe what happens. Have children check their predictions. Circle or check the picture on the chart that is heavier. Follow the same procedure for the rest of the objects on your list. For a challenge, cut the apple in half and repeat the activity.

Change the objects to be weighed and put this activity in your math center for children to explore during free choice time.

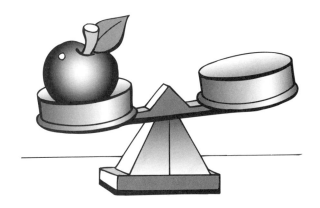

Math

How Many Apples Tall Template

Directions: Photocopy this page three times. Cut out one small apple template, one medium apple template, and one large apple template.

Science

Parts of an Apple Poster

Materials: white posterboard, red bulletin board paper, black, brown, and green construction paper, black marker

 You will want to use this poster to introduce the Big Book on Day One.

To create the poster, draw the outline of a large apple on white posterboard. Cut red chart paper to fit over the outline of the apple. Glue one side of the chart paper down, allowing it to open and reveal the inside of the apple. Use construction paper and cut small black seeds, a brown stem, and a green leaf. Glue these to the posterboard. Label the parts of the apple: *skin, meat, seeds, core, leaf, stem.* After using the poster as part of the prereading activities for the Big Book, allow children to view it during free choice time. Later in the week, ask volunteers to name the parts of the apple.

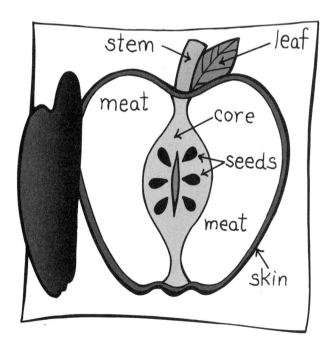

Why Does the Apple Change Color?

Materials: one large apple, two paper plates, one lemon, two index cards, markers

Cut an apple in half. Ask children if they think the apple will change in any way after being cut. Allow them to share their predictions. Record their predictions on chart paper. Then squeeze the juice from the lemon onto one half of the apple. Put it on a paper plate and place an index card on it labeled "with lemon." Place the other half apple on a paper plate and place an index card in front of it labeled, "without lemon." Allow children to make additional predictions. Check the apples at the end of the school day. *What happened to the apple that did not have lemon juice squeezed over it? Why do you think so?*

Explain that the meat of the apple has chemicals inside it that react to the oxygen in the air. When the meat of the apple is exposed to the air, it changes color. The lemon has Vitamin C in it. This slows down the browning reaction of the apple.

Sink or Float?

Materials: clear bowl, water, small apple

Show children a small apple and a clear bowl half-filled with water. Invite them to predict whether the apple will sink or float when placed in the water. *Will the color of the apple make a difference? Will the stem face up or down?* Have children draw what they think will happen to the apple when it is placed in the water. After they draw their predictions, place the apple in the water and observe what happens. Invite children to check their predictions and share their results.

Social Studies

● Johnny Appleseed

Share one of the stories about Johnny Appleseed from the Literature Connection for this theme. Discuss with children that while some of the tales told about John Chapman are probably not true, he was a very kind and gentle man. He loved animals and went out of his way to help others. Explain that John Chapman has become a legend for his kindness and generosity.

Ask children how they can practice the kindness and generosity that John Chapman showed others. Give children possible situations that could happen in the classroom and have them share how they would handle it. For example, *There is only one fire truck, and you and your friend both want to play with it. How can you solve this problem?* Encourage children to think of ways to share and take turns. Remind them that when you share you are being kind to your friends.

Give children other possible classroom and at-home situations that would give them a reason to think about how to be more kind and generous to their friends and family.

● You and your friend both want to play on the computer. What could you do?

● You can jump rope easily, but your friend has trouble jumping rope. What could you do?

● Your friend has too much stuff to carry to the bus. What could you do?

● Your brother/sister can't go out to play until he or she has cleaned his or her room. What could you do?

● Your mom is rushing to get dinner on the table. What could you do?

● Your friend just offered to share his/her snack with you. What could you do?

● Some children are teasing another child on the playground. What could you do?

Literature Connection

Benjamin, A.H. and Gwyneth Williamson. **Little Mouse and Big Red Apple.** Alpharetta, GA: Tiger Tales, 2001.

Bosca, Francesca and Giuliano Ferri. **The Apple King.** New York, NY: North South Books, 2001.

Gibbons, Gail. **Apples.** New York, NY: Holiday House, 2001.

Hall, Zoe. **The Apple Pie Tree.** Jefferson City, MO: Scholastic, 1996.

Hutchins, Pat. **Ten Red Apples.** New York, NY: Greenwillow, 2000.

Kellogg, Steven. **Johnny Appleseed.** Jefferson City, MO: Scholastic, 1988.

Kurtz, Shirley and Cheryl Benner. **Applesauce.** Intercourse, PA: Good Books, 1992.

Le Sieg, Theo. **Ten Apples Up On Top!** New York, NY: Random House, 1961.

Lindbergh, Reeve. **Johnny Appleseed.** Boston, NY: Little Brown and Company, 1990.

Maestro, Betsy and Giulio Maestro. **How Do Apples Grow? (Let's Read and Find Out Book).** New York, NY: Harper Trophy, 1993.

Murphy, Stuart J. **Give Me Half!** Jefferson City, MO: Scholastic, 1996.

Murphy, Stuart J. **Every Buddy Counts.** Jefferson City, MO: Scholastic, 1997.

Rickert, Janet Elizabeth and Pete McGahan. **Russ and the Apple Tree Surprise.** Bethesda, MD: Woodbine House, 1999.

Saunders-Smith, Gail. **From Blossom to Fruit.** Mankato, MN: Pebble Books, 1998.

Wallace, Nancy Elizabeth. **Apples, Apples, Apples.** New York, NY: Winslow Press, 2000.

Harvest

Scope and Sequence

	Sound Identification	Letter Identification	Word Study (high frequency words)	Sequencing	Speaking Skills	Listening Skills	Logical Thinking Skills	Social/Emotional Development	Large Motor Development	Fine Motor Movement
Big Book Introduction					●	●	●			
Revisiting	●	●	●		●	●	●			
Echo Reading	●	●	●		●	●	●			
Choral Reading	●	●	●		●	●	●			
Partner Reading	●	●	●		●	●	●	●		
Poem: "The Cornfield "	●	●	●	●	●	●	●		●	
Song: "Fall is Here!"					●	●	●			
Song: "Growing Pumpkins"					●	●	●	●	●	
Song: "Leaves, Leaves"					●	●	●		●	
Popping Popcorn						●			●	
Whose Got Pumpkin?					●	●		●		
Squirrel Races					●	●	●	●	●	
Falling Leaves					●	●			●	
Marble Paint Leaves						●				●
Scarecrow Art						●				●
Leaf People						●				●
Harvest Feast					●	●		●		
Popcorn Graph					●	●	●			●
Penny Harvest/Sorting						●	●			●
Peanut Story Problems						●	●			●
Five Senses					●	●	●			
Popcorn in Water					●	●	●			
Life Cycle of a Pumpkin					●	●	●	●		
Why Do Leaves Change?					●	●	●			
Penny Harvest					●	●		●		
What Am I Thankful For?					●	●		●		

Weekly Planner

Skills Practice: The letter *Ss* The word *the*	Big Book/ Little Books Pages 74–75	Poetry/ Skills Pages 76	Music and Movement Pages 77–79	Art/Cooking Pages 80–82	Math Pages 83-85	Science Pages 86–87	Social Studies Pages 86–87
Monday	Big Book Introduction: *Fall is Here!*	Poem: "The Cornfield"	Song: "Fall is Here!" Popping Popcorn		Popcorn Graph	Five Senses Popcorn in Water	Penny Harvest Discussion
Tuesday	Revisiting: *Fall is Here!*	Little Book: *Fall is Here!,* the letter *Ss* and the word *the*	Song: "Growing Pumpkins" Whose Got Pumpkin?	Marble Paint Leaves		Life Cycle of a Pumpkin	
Wednesday	Echo Reading: *Fall is Here!*	Poem: "The Cornfield," the letter *Ss*	Squirrel Races	Scarecrow Art	Peanut Story Problems		What Am I Thankful For?
Thursday	Choral Reading: *Fall is Here!*	Little Book: *Fall is Here!,* the word *the*	Song: "Leaves, Leaves" Falling Leaves	Leaf People		Why Do Leaves Change?	
Friday	Partner Reading: *Fall is Here!*			Harvest Feast	Penny Harvest Sort/Count		

Fall is Here!

Name: _____

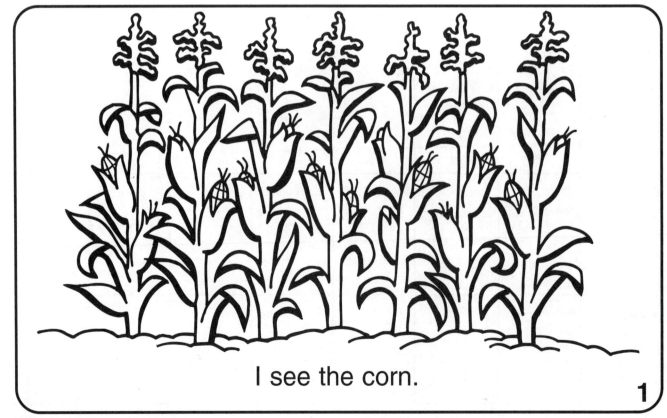

I see the corn.

1

I see the pumpkins.

2

I see the scarecrow.

3

I see the leaves.

4

I see the squirrels hiding nuts.

5

Date _____

Dear Parents,

The changing season brings new challenges and excitement to our classroom. In our upcoming Harvest theme, we will be celebrating the season and sharing all the wonderful gifts that the harvest brings.

Fall is a time to be thankful. In our Apple theme, we shared how to be more kind and giving to our friends and family, and now in the Harvest theme, we would like to extend that generosity to our community. We will be talking about things we are thankful for and how some families are not as fortunate as our own. To help those families, we will be participating in a Penny Harvest. I will be asking children to bring to school some pennies from their piggy banks, the "junk" drawer, under the seat cushions, and so on. We will be collecting them throughout the week. On Friday, we will sort and count the pennies and graph the results. Other classes will be participating in this event as well. We hope to be able to make a substantial donation to the following local organization/ charity: _____.
We would greatly appreciate your contribution to our Penny Harvest.

In another Harvest theme activity, we will be learning about signs of fall. One definite sign of fall is the changing leaves. Please help your child find a leaf with its stem that has fallen from a tree and have him or her bring it to school on _____.
We will be using the leaves for an art project.

    Thank you,

● Beginning the Theme

Use the Supply Request Letterhead provided on page 11 to hand write a supply request letter. You will want to send supply letters home at least one week before you plan to teach the theme. This will give parents time to send in any materials needed. Please remember to use the Student Materials Record to check off which students brought materials for this theme.

This theme requires the following supplies. Ask parents to help supply:

- pumpkin pie
- bread
- corn muffins
- hot air popper
- popcorn kernels for hot air popper
- peanuts in the shell
- apples

Big Book Introduction

● Day One

Prereading

 Begin the theme by sharing the song, "Fall is Here!" found on page 77.

Sing the first verse and then prompt children to brainstorm other signs of fall. *What grows in the field all summer long and is ready to be harvested in the fall?* You might choose to write children's responses on chart paper and re-create the song through class discussion. Sing the song together in its entirety. Briefly review the months of the year and the seasons. Tell children that fall is a time when the weather turns colder, the crops are harvested, and animals and people get ready for winter.

changing leaves

pumpkins growing

squirrels hide nuts

corn on the stalks

apples on the trees

During Reading

Show the front cover and review the title. After reading the title, ask children if they think the signs of fall that they sang about will appear in the story. As you read the book, use the procedures and the questioning techniques presented in the previous themes as a guide for sharing this book with the children. Use your finger to point to each word as you read it. Model one-to-one correspondence and fluency. After reading each page look back to the song chart to check predictions.

Post Reading

Be sure to read the story again without stopping or asking questions. Invite children to read along with you if they choose. Continue pointing to the words as you read. For the remaining days follow the Whole Group Reading Strategies.

Key Vocabulary

Introduce these words throughout the week. Engage children in discussions about the words. When appropriate, provide concrete examples to illustrate the meaning of each word. Use the vocabulary word cards found on page 181 to reinforce the words.

vine	**crop**
harvest	**frost**
donation	**scarecrow**

Whole Group Read

● Day Two

Revisiting: Fall is Here!

Revisit the signs of fall song chart you created yesterday. *Does anyone have anything else they would like to add to the chart? What signs of fall did you see yesterday after school?* Allow children to add new fall signs to the chart. Introduce and write the word *the* on the board, emphasizing the letters as you write them. Point out that the word *the* has three letters, but it has only two sounds. The letters *t* and *h* work together to make the beginning sound. Say the word and point to the letters as you read. Tell children that while you are reading, you want them to listen for the word *the*. When they hear it or see it, they can tug on one ear. Revisit the story and frame the word *the* as you read it. Invite children to read the book along with you. Be sure to use your finger or a pointer to demonstrate one-to-one correspondence.

● Day Three

Echo Reading: Fall is Here!

Have children use their Little Books as they echo you. Encourage them to use their finger to match the written word to the spoken word as they are reading. After reading the book, frame the letter *Ss* and have children point to it in their Little Books. Invite them to echo you as you say the letter and the sound.

Encourage children to think of other words that begin with the letter *Ss*. Write the words on chart paper. Be sure to use two colors, one for the beginning sound, another for the remaining sounds.

After echo reading, have children return to their seats and give them a few minutes to write their name on the book and color the pictures. Revisit the book page-by-page. Invite children to use their favorite color to find and circle the letter *Ss* and to circle the high-frequency word *the*. Collect the books for Days Four and Five.

● Day Four

Choral Reading: Fall is Here!

Distribute the Little Books and read aloud together. Encourage children to point to each word as they read it. Focus on the high-frequency word *see*. Help children read it on each page. Watch for the left-to-right progression. Collect the books for Day Five.

● Day Five

Partner Reading: Fall is Here!

As children read together, use the checklist on page 184 or make anecdotal notes about students' individual concepts about print skills. See Marie Clay's *An Observation Survey of Early Literacy Achievement* for a complete listing of print skills.

Poetry

On Day One of reading the poem, you will want to focus on the letter/sound *Ss*. In subsequent readings, you can revisit the high-frequency words *and/the*.

The Cornfield

After growing all summer	*(Crouch down and wrap your hands around your knees and slowly rise up, stretching your arms above your head.)*
In the rain and the sun,	*(Wiggle your fingers above your head to your waist to show rain and make a big circle above your head to show the sun.)*
The corn can be harvested,	*(Pull an ear of corn from the stalk)*
Oh what fun!	*(Wiggle dance)*
It is safe for right now	*(Stand tall like a stalk of corn)*
For the scarecrow, you see,	*(Stand with your arms bent by your ears like a scarecrow)*
Is busy keeping crows away from the seeds!	*(Flap arms)*

Music and Movement

Fall is Here!
(Sung to the tune of "Wheels on the Bus")

The changing leaves tell us fall is here!
Fall is here, fall is here.
The changing leaves tell us fall is here,
What other signs are near?

The tall, yellow corn tells us fall is here!
Fall is here, fall is here.
The tall, yellow corn tells us fall is here,
What other signs are near?

The orange, round pumpkins tell us fall is here!
Fall is here, fall is here.
The orange, round pumpkins tell us fall is here,
What other signs are near?

The shiny, sweet apples tell us fall is here!
Fall is here, fall is here.
The shiny, sweet apples tell us fall is here,
What other signs are near?

The frosty chill tells us fall is here!
Fall is here, fall is here.
The frosty chill tells us fall is here,
What other signs are near?

The squirrels hiding nuts tells us fall is here!
Fall is here, fall is here.
The squirrels hiding nuts tells us fall is here,
What other signs are near?

Growing Pumpkins
(Sung to the tune of "If You're Happy and You Know It")
If you choose to sing the song without the picture props, (see page 88) you can add the movements below each verse.

If you're a pumpkin seed, clap your hands.
If you're a pumpkin seed, clap your hands.
The pumpkin seed will grow
And its flower soon will show.
If you're a pumpkin seed, clap your hands.
  (Crouch down, hugging your knees. Stand slowly opening your arms wide.)

If you're a pumpkin flower, clap your hands.
If you're a pumpkin flower, clap your hands.
The flower wilts away
But a pumpkin's on its way.
If you're a pumpkin flower, clap your hands.
  (Wiggle-wilt to the floor.)

If you're a growing pumpkin, clap your hands.
If you're a growing pumpkin, clap your hands.
You'll grow strong on the vine
And you'll look mighty fine.
If you're a growing pumpkin, clap your hands.
  (Make a small ball with your hands in front of you and have it grow bigger and bigger.)

If you're a big, round pumpkin, clap your hands.
If you're a big, round pumpkin, clap your hands.
Time to cut you from the vine
Take you home and make you mine.
If you're a big, round pumpkin, clap your hands.
  (Stretch arms out wide. Bend down on one knee and cut the pumpkin from the vine. Pick it up with both hands and carry it home.)

Music and Movement

 This song can accompany the large motor activity, **Falling Leaves,** found on page 79. You might also choose to write this song on chart paper and have children frame the letter *Ss* and any high-frequency words they know.

Leaves, Leaves
(Sung to the tune of "Skip to My Lou")

Leaves, leaves

Yellow, red, and green.

Leaves, leaves,

Falling from the trees.

Leaves, leaves,

Piles to my knees.

Signs of fall for you to see.

● Popping Popcorn

 This large motor activity should accompany the **Five Senses** lesson found on page 86 of this theme.

After popping popcorn in the hot air popper, have children mimic popping popcorn. Start by crouching down like a ball and hopping a little at first. *It is getting hot in this popcorn popper. I am really starting to feel the heat.* Then hop a little faster. *I'm not sure how much more heat I can take.* Continue to hop faster until finally, you pop! Animate the pop by jumping up high and stretching your arms above your head.

Whose Got Pumpkin?

Materials: CD or audiotape player, orange button or plastic cube, blindfold

Have children sit in a circle. Invite one child to be the "guesser." This child sits in the middle of the circle, blindfolded. Hand one child in the circle a small orange button or plastic cube to represent the pumpkin. Play music and have children pass the "pumpkin" around the circle. When the music stops, the guesser has three chances to guess who is holding the pumpkin. The person holding the pumpkin becomes the next guesser. If that person has already had a turn, the guesser becomes the person to his or her right.

Music and Movement

● Squirrel Races

Materials: One brown sock for each child (plus a few extra), pylons

You can play this game indoors or outside. Divide the children into two teams. Ball up the brown socks and scatter them about the grass or floor. Talk with children about how squirrels gather nuts for the winter season. *Why do they gather nuts? How do they carry them? Where do they hide them?* Explain to children that they are going to be squirrels. The socks represent nuts and the pylons are trees. One child from each team will crawl on hands and knees to a nut. They will put the nut under their chin and crawl on all fours to their tree. The next team member can begin once the nut has been placed under the tree. The team that has the most nuts by their tree within the time limit is the winner. Allow time for each child to have one turn. Mix up the teams and play again!

● Falling Leaves

Explain to children that water is carried from the stem to the leaf to help keep the leaf alive. In the fall the stem, where it is connected to the branch, gets bigger. Water can't pass through to get to the leaf. Eventually the leaf dries and is blown away or falls from the tree.

Have children pretend they are leaves that are about to be blown from a tree. Tell them to use their legs as the stems hanging onto the tree and mimic being pulled by the wind. Eventually children will release their legs and swing their arms as if they are floating through the air. Children can float around the room and slowly come to rest on the ground. Repeat the activity allowing children to float in the air, sway in the wind, and fall straight to the ground.

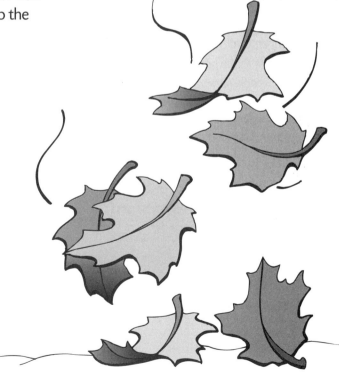

Art/Cooking

● Marble Paint Leaves

Materials: red, orange, green, yellow, purple, and brown poster paint, marbles, small bowls, plastic spoons, cardboard box, leaf template, 9" x 12" white construction paper.

Use the pattern on page 82 to make a leaf template on heavy card stock. Have a parent volunteer trace the leaf on white 9" x 12" construction paper, one for each student in your class. Prepare these ahead of time.

Invite children to sit in a circle or gather them around the table as you model the activity. *Write your name on the back of the paper and place it with the leaf print facing up in the cardboard box. Using the spoon, roll the marble in the bowl of paint and pick it up with the spoon. Place the marble on the paper and put the spoon back in the bowl. Carefully pick up the box and roll the marble around by gently moving the box. Pick up the marble and clean your fingers and the marble in a bowl of fresh water. Return the marble to the paint and choose another color. With a different spoon, remove the marble and repeat the process with another color. Continue until your leaf is full of colored lines. Take the paper out of the box and place it in the drying rack.*

 Children will use the product of this activity in the social studies lesson **What Am I Thankful For** found on page 87.

● Scarecrow Art

Materials: 12" x 18" yellow and orange construction paper, 9" x 12" brown, white, black, red, blue construction paper, hay (optional), glue

Create the pieces you will need for each student.

 1 orange hat (8½" tall by 12" wide)

 1 yellow circle (10½" diameter)

 2 white ovals and 2 black circles (eyes)

 8-10 pieces of ripped brown paper (hair)

 1 orange triangle (nose)

 1 red mouth

 1 blue collar

Since there are lots of pieces to this project, you may want to have all of them prepared ahead of time. This activity works best when each child has his or her own gallon-size plastic bag with all the pieces needed to complete the project. Model the step-by-step process and guide children through this activity.

Take the yellow face out of the plastic bag and put your name on one side. On that same side glue the blue collar to the bottom of the scarecrow. Turn it over. To make the eyes, glue the two white circles near the top of the yellow circle. Glue one black circle on each white circle to finish the eyes. Tear the brown paper for hair and glue it to either side of the scarecrow's face. Add the orange triangle nose and red mouth. Finally, glue the hat on top.

Art/Cooking

For an added touch, glue some hay to the hat to make it look more authentic. After the scarecrows are dry, use a marker to add children's names on the hat. Display them in your classroom or in the hallway.

● Leaf People

Materials: white 12" x 18" construction paper, variety of colored 12" x 18" construction paper, glue, googly eyes

Use the letter on page 73 to ensure that children bring a leaf to school to complete this activity. You may want to have on hand extra leaves for those children who forget their leaf. Review with children the parts of the body. Point out your arms, legs, hands, feet, head, eyes, nose, and mouth. Explain to children that you are going to draw a self-portrait with the leaf as your body and the stem as your neck.

You might choose to sing "Head, Shoulders, Knees and Toes" from the *Friends and Me* theme or to do the "Hokey Pokey."

On a 12" x 18" sheet of white construction paper, glue the leaf with the stem pointing up. Above the stem draw a circle for your head and add eyes, a nose, and a mouth. It is fun to use googly eyes, too. Then add arms, hands, legs, and feet.

As children finish their picture, bubble cut it for them and write their name on the front. Have them choose a sheet of 12" x 18" colored construction paper and glue their leaf portrait on the colored paper. After they are dry, bubble cut again following the original form. Display in your classroom or hallway.

● Harvest Feast

Always check for food sensitivities and allergies before serving food to children.

Materials: napkins, small plates, cups for water or apple juice

Use the Supply Request Letterhead provided on page 11 to hand write a supply request letter. Ask parents to send a harvest snack to share with the class. This might include: apples, pumpkin pie, corn bread, popcorn and so on. If other classes have participated in the Penny Harvest, include them in the feast. Plan to have your feast in the multi-purpose room or set up the feast in two different classrooms and allow children to visit and feast with their friends. It is also a great opportunity to invite other teachers, staff, and the principal.

Art/Cooking

Marble Paint Leaf

Math

● Popcorn Graph

Materials: yellow, orange, and brown construction paper cut into 6" x 2" strips, tape

Prepare ahead of time yellow, orange, and brown construction paper cut into 4" x 2" strips. The yellow will represent buttered popcorn, orange will represent cheese popcorn, and brown will represent caramel popcorn. Invite children to choose their favorite and to take a corresponding strip. Have children sit in groups according to their favorite kind of popcorn. Show children how to make a paper chain and link the strips (use tape to hold the sides together). When finished, find a place on the wall to hang the chains. Compare the lengths. *Which flavor has the most? Least? Are any the same?* After counting each flavor, *What numbers were odd? Even?* Record your findings on chart paper. Leave the paper chains hanging for children to revisit on their own.

● Penny Harvest: Sorting and Counting

Materials: pennies, empty egg cartons

 Use this activity after children have collected pennies for the **Penny Harvest** activity found on page 87.

Model for children how to sort the pennies into groups of ten, using an egg carton counter. Cut off two adjoining cups from an egg carton and discard them. This will leave ten cups intact. On the inside wall of each cup, write multiples of ten (10, 20, 30, and so on, to 100.) Model how to touch count ten pennies and put them in the 10 cup of the egg

carton counter. Touch count ten more pennies and add them to the 20 cup of the egg carton. Continue until all ten cups in the egg carton counter are full. Count by tens showing children ten sets of ten equals 100, or one dollar. Empty the egg carton counter into a large bucket and on chart paper add one tally mark. Explain that this is how you will keep track of the number of dollars you have "harvested." Each tally mark will equal one dollar.

Pair children. Give each pair an egg carton counter and a cup full of pennies. Remind them to put ten pennies in each of the egg counter cups and then to bring it to you to empty into the bucket. They can then add a tally to the chart.

When all the pennies have been counted, invite children to sit in front of the chart. Together, count the tallies. If other classes have participated in the Penny Harvest, create a wall graph in the lobby of the school with each classroom listed and the number of dollars each class collected. In your next newsletter, be sure to inform parents of the total dollar amount collected and the charity or organization to which you donated the money.

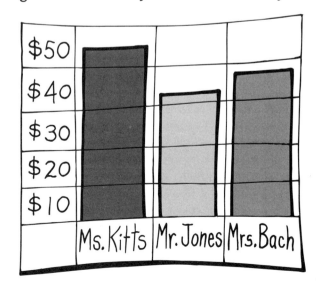

Math

● Peanuts Story Problems

Materials: peanuts in the shell (see Supply Request on page 73), small plastic bowls, storyboard picture

Caution: *Some children can be dangerously allergic to peanuts. Even handling peanuts or something that has come into contact with a peanut may cause an allergic reaction. Always check for food sensitivities and allergies before serving food to children. You can modify the activity to use a different type of food or plastic interlocking cubes if a child in your classroom has an allergy to peanuts.*

Photocopy the storyboard on page 85, one for each student. Allow children to color the tree and instruct them to color the boy squirrel gray and the girl squirrel brown. Place a bowl full of peanuts or peanut substitutes in the middle of each table. After children have colored their storyboard, invite them to give each squirrel five peanuts. Between the squirrels there is a total of ten peanuts. Tell children to listen carefully to the story of Sebastian and Camille.

Sebastian and Camille have gathered some peanuts to store for the winter. We are going to use their peanuts to solve some story problems. First check to make sure Sebastian and Camille each have five peanuts. Listen carefully and follow along with me.

*Take two peanuts from Sebastian and put them in the tree. Take one peanut from Camille and put it in the tree. How many peanuts are now in the tree? Let's touch count and see. Clap your hands if you have three peanuts in the tree. Good job!

Be sure to walk around and help those that are having difficulty.

*We have three peanuts in the tree, take two more peanuts from Camille and put them in the tree. How many peanuts are in the tree now? Let's touch count and see. If you have five peanuts in the tree, snap your fingers.

Continue with this format until all the peanuts are in the tree. When all ten peanuts are in the tree, divide them between the squirrels and repeat. If your students are able to do subtraction, follow this format.

*We now have ten peanuts in the tree. Take one peanut from the tree and give it to Camille. We had ten peanuts, but we gave one to Camille, how many do we have left? Very good, ten peanuts take away one peanut leaves us with nine peanuts.

Continue until all the peanuts are distributed between the squirrels. When you are satisfied with the children's practice with simple addition and/or subtraction, allow them to eat the peanuts.

Math

Math Storyboard

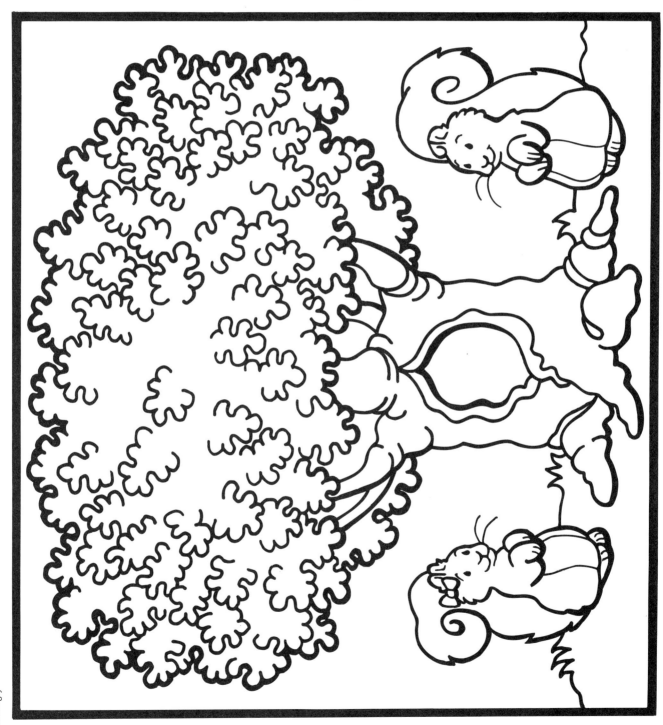

Science

● Five Senses

Always check for food sensitivities and allergies before serving food to children.

Materials: butcher paper, markers, popcorn, hot air popper

 You might choose to introduce this activity by singing the "We Use Five Senses" song from the *Friends and Me* theme on page 21.

Ahead of time, prepare on butcher paper a five senses poster. Create two columns. Label the first column *Corn Kernel* and the other column *Popcorn*. On the left side of the graph draw and label each of the five senses. Ask children where popcorn comes from and how it is made. Explain that each kernel has a little bit of water in it and when the water gets hot enough—Pop! *Today you are going to investigate both corn kernels and popcorn using your five senses.* Show the poster to children. *What does a corn kernel look like? Does it make a sound? What does a corn kernel smell like? Do you think it has a taste? What does it feel like?* Record children's responses on chart paper.

Set up the hot air popper. Remind children to think about their five senses as the popcorn is popping. Review the five senses again with the popcorn. *What does popcorn look like? What did it sound like while it was popping? How does popcorn smell? How does popcorn taste and feel?* When the poster is complete, share the tasty treat!

● Popcorn in Water

Materials: small baby food jar, popcorn kernels, water, paper towel

Fill a small glass jar almost full of popcorn kernels. Add water to the jar, just below the rim. Place the jar on a paper towel. Ask children to make predictions about what might happen. Review your discussion of why popcorn pops. Allow the popcorn to sit for an hour or two. Encourage children to keep an eye on the experiment. At the end of the day revisit the experiment. What happened? (The popcorn should have spilled over the top of the glass onto the paper towel.) Ask children to share why they think this happened. Explain that the kernels in the jar absorbed the water, similar to the way a sponge does. Just like a sponge gets bigger when it is wet, so do the popcorn kernels.

● Life Cycle of a Pumpkin

Materials: several copies of the Life Cycle of a Pumpkin (page 88), butcher paper, construction paper

Children will learn the stages of the pumpkin's life cycle from seed to fruit. Photocopy the pictures on page 88. Copy several of each stage, enough so that each child in your class can hold one of the stages. Color the pictures, glue them onto colored construction paper, and laminate for durability.

 Copy the song, "Growing Pumpkins" (page 77) on butcher paper.

Keep one of each picture for discussion. Display the pictures out of sequence on the board. Ask children which picture they think is first in the life cycle of a pumpkin. Guide children through the stages, moving the pictures to show the correct sequence of events.

Science•Social Studies

Invite children to sit in a circle and randomly distribute the pumpkin life cycle pictures. Remove the pictures from the board and tape them on the song chart. Have children explain their picture and its part in the life cycle. Tell them that if their picture matches the verse you are singing, they are to clap along with that verse. After singing, invite children to exchange their picture for another and sing the song again.

● Why Do Leaves Change Color?

Explain to children that in the spring and summer months, leaves contain a pigment called *chlorophyll.* Chlorophyll gives the leaves their green color. In the fall, the leaves do not make as much chlorophyll so the green color disappears, and other colors such as yellows, reds, and oranges appear. Take the children on a nature walk to view the beautiful colors of the season. When you return to the classroom, invite children to sit in a circle and have them share what they saw and their favorite color leaf.

Social Studies

Penny Harvest

Materials: chart paper

Share with children that this season is a time to be thankful. Help children to brainstorm things for which they are thankful and record their responses on chart paper. You can prompt children to include

family, friends, food, shelter, clothes, pets, and so on. Explain that not all families have an abundance of the necessities listed on the chart and often need help. Tell children that as a class, along with other classes that will be participating, they will be collecting pennies to donate to those families that need help. This will be called a *Penny Harvest.* Tell children when they go home to ask their parents if they can have the pennies from their piggy bank, find the pennies in the "junk" drawer, and ask if mom and dad can empty the pennies from their pockets, too. Photocopy the note on page 73 to send home to parents.

 Use the **Sorting and Counting** activity on page 83 after you have completed the Penny Harvest.

What Am I Thankful For?

Materials: chart of items for which we are thankful, Marble Paint Leaves, scissors

 Use the **Marble Paint Leaves** you created to give this Social Studies activity flair!

Have children cut out the leaves they painted in the Marble Paint Leaves activity. On the leaves, help them to write something for which they are thankful. Refer to the chart you created on Monday when you introduced the Penny Harvest to help spark ideas. Be sure children's names appear on the front of the leaf. Create a tree for your bulletin board and hang the leaves or tape them around the Penny Harvest graph. (See page 83)

Science

Life Cycle of a Pumpkin

Literature Connection

Brisson, Pat and Bob Barner. **Benny's Pennies.** Westminister, MD: Bantam Doubleday Dell Books for Young Readers, 1993.

DePaola, Tommie. **The Popcorn Book.** New York, NY: Holiday House, Inc., 1978.

Ehlert, Lois. **Nuts to You!** Jefferson City, MO: Scholastic, 1993.

Hall, Zoe and Shari Halpern. **It's Pumpkin Time!** Jefferson City, MO: Scholastic, 1994.

Kroll, Steven. **The Biggest Pumpkin Ever.** Jefferson City, MO: Scholastic, 1984.

Maas, Robert. **When Autumn Comes.** Jefferson City, MO: Scholastic, 1990.

Maestro, Betsy and Loretta Krupinski. **Why Do Leaves Change Colors?** New York, NY: HarperCollins, 1994.

Muldrow, Diane and Jill Dubin. **We Love Fall!** Jefferson City, MO: Scholastic, 1997.

Robbins, Ken. **Autumn Leaves.** Jefferson City, MO: Scholastic, 1998.

Rockwell, Anne and Lizzy Rockwell. **Apples and Pumpkins.** New York, NY: Aladdin Paperbacks, 1994.

Rockwell, Anne and Megan Halsey. **Pumpkin Day, Pumpkin Night.** Jefferson City, MO: Scholastic, 1999.

Rylant, Cynthia and Lauren Stringer. **Scarecrow.** Orlando, FL: Harcourt Brace & Company, 1998.

Titherington, Jeanne. **Pumpkin, Pumpkin.** New York, NY: Mulberry Books, 1986.

White, Linda and Megan Lloyd. **Too Many Pumpkins.** New York, NY: Holiday House, 1996.

Williams, Linda and Megan Lloyd. **The Little Old Lady Who Was Not Afraid of Anything**. New York, NY: HarperCollins, 1986.

Winkelman, Barbara and Kristen Kest. **Flying Squirrel at Acorn Place.** Jefferson City, MO: Scholastic, 1998.

Snow

Scope and Sequence

	Sound Identification	Letter Identification	Word Study (high frequency words)	Sequencing	Speaking Skills	Listening Skills	Logical Thinking Skills	Social / Emotional Development	Large Motor Development	Fine Motor Movement
Big Book Introduction					●	●	●			
Revisiting	●	●	●	●	●	●	●			
Echo Reading	●	●	●	●	●	●	●			
Choral Reading	●	●	●	●	●	●	●			
Partner Reading	●	●	●	●	●	●	●	●		
Poem: "Snowgirl"	●	●	●		●	●		●		
Poem: "What's a Pair?"						●				
Song: "Snow, Snow"					●	●				
Song: "New Mittens"					●	●				
Balloon Toss					●	●	●	●	●	
Getting Dressed					●	●		●	●	
Hot Chocolate Rap					●	●				
Snowman				●		●				●
Watercolor Mittens				●	●	●	●			●
Tortilla Snowballs				●		●		●		●
Hot Chocolate								●		
Snowman Match						●	●			●
What Comes in Pairs					●	●	●			
Mittens or Gloves Graph					●	●		●		●
Patterning					●	●	●			
Marshmallow Math						●	●			●
Time to Change					●	●	●			
Telephone					●	●		●		
Change Experiment					●	●	●			
Smiles are Contagious								●		
How Have You Changed?				●	●	●		●		
Change the Routine					●	●		●		
Class Book							●	●		

Weekly Planner

Skills Practice The letter *Mm* The word *My*	Big Book/ Little Books Pages 97–98	Poetry/ Skills Pages 99	Music and Movement Pages 100–101	Art/Cooking Pages 102–104	Math Pages 105–110	Science Page 111	Social Studies Page 112
Monday	Big Book Introduction: *My Snowman*	Poem: "Snowgirl"	Song: "Snow, Snow"	Snowman	Snowman Match	Time to Change	Smiles Are Contagious How Have You Changed? (At home activity)
Tuesday	Revisiting: *My Snowman*	Little Book: *My Snowman*, the letter *Mm*, and the word *my*	Song and Movement: "Getting Dressed"	Tortilla Snowballs	Mittens or Gloves Graph		Change the Routine
Wednesday	Echo Reading: *My Snowman*	Poem: "What's a Pair?," the letter *Mm*	Song: "New Mittens"	Watercolor Mittens	Patterning What Comes in Pairs?	Telephone	
Thursday	Choral Reading: *My Snowman*	Little Book: *My Snowman*, the word *my*	Balloon Toss	Cut out Watercolor Mittens and glue cotton		Change Experiment	Class Book
Friday	Partner Reading: *My Snowman*		Song: "Hot Chocolate Rap"	Hot Chocolate	Marshmallow Math		How Have You Changed? Presentation

My Snowman

Name: _____

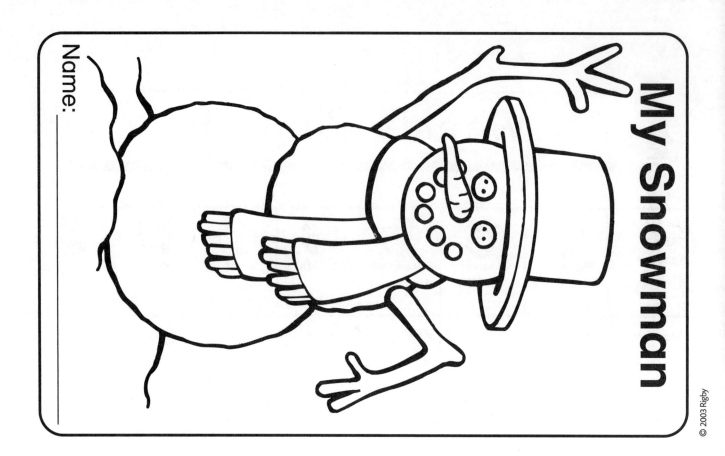

My snowman has a hat.

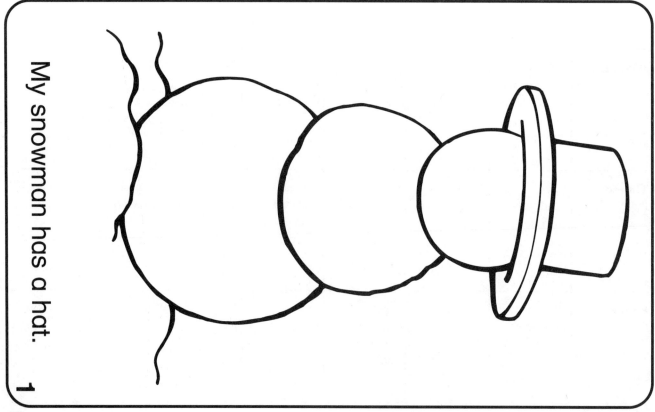

1

My snowman has
button eyes.

2

My snowman has
a carrot nose.

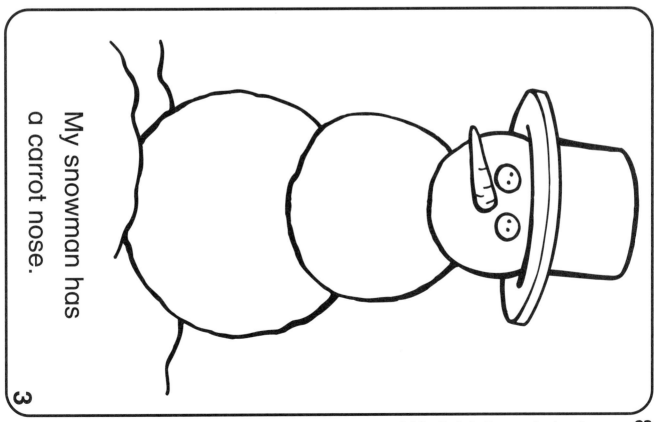

3

My snowman has
a long scarf.

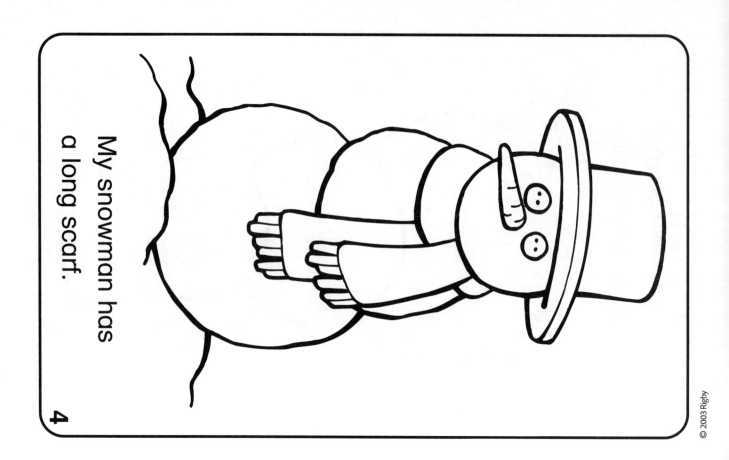

4

My snowman has
a big smile.

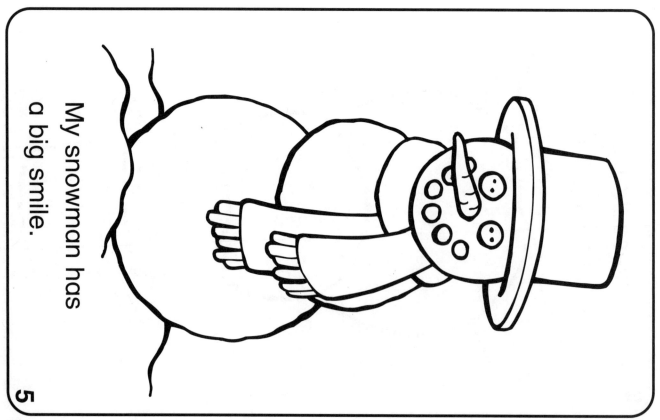

5

My snowman has
two stick arms.

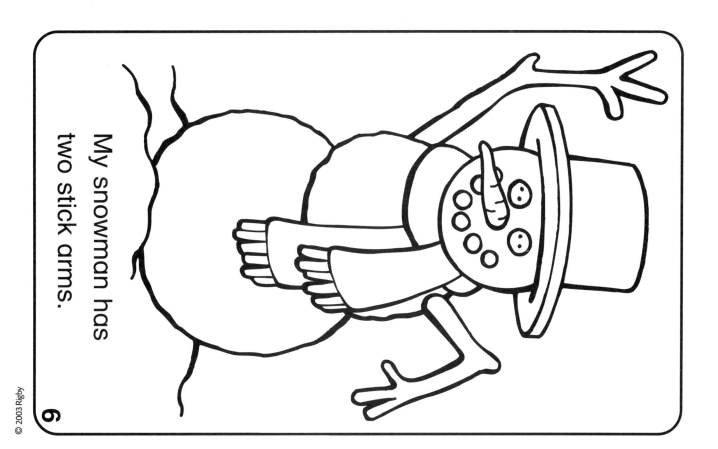

6

My snowman has melted!

7

Date _____

Dear Parents,

The season is changing, and we are going to study one of winter's most wonderful offerings–snow! We will also study change: seasons, time, flowers, snow melting to water, and so on. You can help reinforce the concepts we are exploring at school by pointing out changes that occur over time. You might point out how cookie dough changes after being in the oven or how the family's clothing choice changes with the seasons.

As a culminating activity, we will be sharing how each of us has changed! Please help your child create a "How Have You Changed?" timeline. Show the following stages of your child's life by taping or pasting childhood pictures onto construction paper or posterboard. Label the pictures with these captions: Me at Birth, Me at One Year, Me at Two Years, Me at Three Years, Me at Four Years, Me at Five Years, Me at Six Years. Allow your child to practice presenting his or her timeline to you. Please send the timeline to school on _____ as we will be sharing them with our friends.

Thank you,

© 2003 Rigby

● Beginning the Theme

Use the Supply Request Letterhead provided on page 11 to hand write a supply request letter. You will want to send supply letters home at least one week before you plan to teach the theme. This will give parents time to send in any materials needed. Please remember to use the Student Materials Record to check off which students brought materials for this theme. This theme requires the following supplies. Ask parents to help supply:

- 1 bag of mini-marshmallows
- 1 container of instant hot chocolate
- 1 package of polystyrene cups
- 1 package of soft tortillas
- 1 sandwich bag of diced celery
- 1 tub of soft cream cheese
- 1 package of shredded cheddar cheese
- 1 sandwich bag of diced carrots

© 2003 Rigby

Big Book Introduction

● Day One

Prereading

Show the front cover of *My Snowman* and have children share their experiences with building a snowman. *Who helped you? What did you use for the eyes, nose, mouth, and arms? How long did your snowman last?* Using your finger as a pointer, read the title. Invite children to share predictions about this snowman. *What do you think we will read about this snowman?*

During Reading

Turn to the first page. *What feature does this snowman have?* As you read, use a pointer or your finger to model correspondence of the written word to the spoken word. Follow the same pattern of questioning for the remaining pages.

   As you read the book, use the procedures and questioning techniques presented in the previous units as a guide for sharing this book with the children. Before you turn to the last page, ask children, *What else could the snowman have? What might happen to the snowman?* Allow children to share their predictions. Read the last page with great expression. Make note of the exclamation point. Explain to children that an exclamation point means you need to read with more expression. Invite children to echo you as you read with expression.

Post Reading

Be sure to read the story again without stopping or asking questions. Invite children to read along with you if they choose. Continue pointing to the words as you read. For the remaining days, follow the Whole Group Reading Strategies.

Whole Group Reading Strategies

● Day Two

Revisiting: My Snowman

As a group, read the story together. Use your finger to model one-to-one correspondence. Focus on the letter *Mm*. After reading, invite volunteers to frame the letter *Mm*. Brainstorm words that begin with the letter *Mm*. Be sure to use two different colors when writing the words on chart paper. Use one color for the beginning sound and another color for the remaining letters.

Look at the picture and discuss how with each page, the snowman is closer to being complete. Allow children to return to their seats and color the pictures. Read the story together. Have children find and circle the high-frequency word *My* and the letter *Mm*.

● Day Three

Echo Reading: My Snowman

Using the Big Book, have children echo you as you read the story. In doing this, you are helping to build confidence and improve fluency. Focus on the high-frequency word *My*. Invite volunteers to frame the word. Add the word to your word wall. Encourage children to refer to the word wall when they are writing in their journals.

● Day Four

Choral Reading: My Snowman

Using the Big Book, invite a volunteer to point to the words as children choral read. Choral reading allows children to participate in a risk-free environment. Revisit punctuation and the difference between a period and an exclamation point. Distribute the Little Books and read the story again together. Remind children to attend to punctuation. Collect the books for Day Five.

● Day Five

Partner Reading: My Snowman

Use the partner sticks to match children up or pair them as you see fit. As children read together, use the checklist on page 184 or make anecdotal notes about students' individual concepts about print skills. See Marie Clay's *An Observation Survey of Early Literacy Achievement* for a complete listing of print skills.

Key Vocabulary

Introduce these words throughout the week. Engage children in discussions about the words. When appropriate provide tangible examples to illustrate the meaning of each word. Use the vocabulary word cards found on page 182 to reinforce the words.

pair	mittens	contagious
change	gloves	scarf

Poetry

After reading this poem ask children to share what the end of the poem means to them. You might prompt their thinking by asking the following questions. *Is this a happy or sad snowgirl? Why do you think she feels that way?* Help them to understand that the snowgirl was made with love so she always wore a big smile. Invite volunteers to find the letter *Mm* and any high-frequency words they know.

 Read this poem as part of the math lesson found on page 105 of this theme.

What's a Pair?

I put it in my pocket.

I thought I felt it there.

I cannot find my mitten–

I've looked everywhere!

What good is just one mitten?

They always come in pairs.

Losing just one mitten,

simply isn't fair.

Snowgirl

I rolled my little snowball
across the quiet ground.
I tried to make it perfect,
big and fat and round.
I made another snowball
and rolled that one, too.
When set upon the other,
my snowgirl grew and grew.
I gave her a straw hat
and flowers for her eyes,
an orange carrot for a nose,
a smile big and wide.

My snowgirl stayed awhile,
through the bitter cold and wind.
Her smile never fading,
True smiles never end.

Music and Movement

Snow, Snow

*(Sung to the tune of
"Oh Dear, What Can the Matter Be?")*

Snow, snow,
   flakes floating swiftly down.
Snow, snow,
   falling all over town.
Snow, snow,
   always white never brown.
Can't wait to go out and play–Hooray!

New Mittens

(Sung to the tune of Down In the Valley)

I've lost my new mittens,
so warm and so snug.
If you help me find them,
I'll give you a hug.

Using magnetic letters make the word *snug*. Use one color for the consonant blend and another color for the rime. Point out the onset (beginning sound) and the rime (ending sound.) Remove the *sn* and ask, *What letter is needed to make the word hug?* Have other letters available and invite volunteers to make new words. Add these letters to your writing or reading center for independent practice.

Tip: A cookie sheet makes a great tablet for magnetic letters.

● Balloon Toss

Materials: balloon, children's gloves or mittens

This is a perfect game for days when it is too cold to go outside. Have half the class get their gloves or mittens. (You will probably have to play this game another day so the other children can use their mittens.) Put the mittens in a bag and have the children sit in a circle. Walk around the circle and have each child take out one mitten or glove. Instruct children to put their mitten on. If there is an odd number, squeeze your hand into the extra mitten. Instruct children to look for their matching glove or mitten.

Once everyone has found his or her partner, have children stand up and then explain the rules of the game. Hand the balloon to one of the children. That person has to bat the balloon to his or her mitten/ glove partner. The partner can bat the balloon to anyone, but the next person has to bat the balloon to his or her mitten/glove partner. You might need to walk children through a sample round. The goal is to see how long they can keep the balloon in the air while batting it to the right person. For a challenge, have them use only the hand that is wearing the glove or mitten.

Hot Chocolate Rap

Hot chocolate, hot chocolate,
   so warm and so sweet.
On a cold winter's day, it's really a treat.
Add marshmallows–Yum!
There's nothing better.
Hot chocolate tastes great in snowy weather.

Music and Movement

● Getting Dressed

Materials: winter clothes such as snowpants, boots, hats, scarves, mittens/gloves, jackets

As you sing, act out each of the movements: putting on snowpants, strapping on boots, zipping up a jacket, putting on a hat, and slipping on mittens. In your dramatic play area, provide children with some of the items in the song, and you might even add some items (scarves, thick socks, earmuffs). Encourage children to use these winter items when playing.

You might also choose to write this song on chart paper and have children frame the high-frequency words they know. The word high-frequency *my* is repeated frequently in this song and having volunteers frame the word provides great reinforcement.

Getting Dressed
(Sung to the tune of
"The Bear Went Over the Mountain")

First I can put on my snowpants.
First I can put on my snowpants.
First I can put on my snowpants.
Then I strap on my boots.
Then I strap on my boots.
Then I strap on my boots.
First I put on my snowpants.
Then I strap on my boots.

Now I can zip up my jacket.
Now I can zip up my jacket.
Now I can zip up my jacket.
And put on my nice, warm hat.
And put on my nice, warm hat.
And put on my nice, warm hat.
Now I can zip up my jacket.
And put on my nice, warm hat.

At last I slip on my mittens.
At last I slip on my mittens.
At last I slip on my mittens.
And go outside to play.
And go outside to play.
And go outside to play.
At last I slip on my mittens-
I LOVE a snowy day!

● Snowman

Materials: tagboard, 12" x 18" white construction paper, 9" x 12" colored construction paper: black, blue, orange, red, yellow, brown

Make tagboard templates of the following items:

 Circle (white, 9" diameter)

 Hat (black, 7½" base)

 Scarf (blue, approximately 2" wide by 10" long)

 Carrot nose (orange triangle approximately 4" tall)

 Twig arms (brown, 12" x 2" strips)

Children will also need:

 6 black circles (1" diameter)

 2 colored circles (2" diameter)

Prepare one tracing set for every table. Model for children how to make the snowman. This can be completed as a whole group activity. Fold the 12" x 18" white paper in half and trace the circle so that it slightly overlaps the folded edge. Keeping the paper folded, cut out the circle. Be sure not to cut on the folded edge. This will keep the snowman together. Then trace the hat, scarf, and carrot nose on the appropriate construction paper and cut them out. To make the arms, show children how to fringe the ends of the brown paper to resemble a twig. When all of the pieces have been traced and cut out, you can assemble the snowman.

On one side of the snowman write your name. On that same side, glue the brown twigs so when the paper is turned over it looks like the arms are sticking out of the snowman. Turn the snowman over and glue the black hat to the top. Then glue the scarf where the two circles are connected. Next add the carrot nose, the eyes, mouth, and buttons.

If you are doing this as a whole group activity, walk children through each step. Display snowmen in your classroom.

Art/Cooking

● Watercolor Mittens

Materials: mitten template on page 104, tagboard, 12" x 18" white construction paper, watercolor paints, cotton balls, glue, scissors, yarn, tape

 Before painting, follow the **Patterning** math lesson found on page 106.

Create a mitten template on tagboard from the outline on page 104. Prior to the activity, trace two mittens on one 12" x 18" sheet of white construction paper. Depending on the level and ability of your students, model for them how to paint an *ab* or *abc* pattern on the mittens. Be sure to do the same pattern on each mitten since they are a pair.

The following day have children cut out the mittens. Show them how to pull cotton balls apart to create "fuzz" and glue to the bottom of each mitten. When the glue has dried, tape a six to eight inch piece of yarn to the back of each mitten to connect them. Display in your classroom or in the hallway.

● Tortilla Snowballs

Always check for food sensitivities and allergies before serving food to children.

Materials: small tortillas, soft cream cheese, diced carrots and celery, shredded cheddar cheese, popsicle sticks, small plastic bowls, paper plates

Divide the cream cheese, carrots, celery, and cheddar cheese among the tables. Give each child a "snowball" (tortilla) and a popsicle stick for spreading. Show them how to spread the "snow" and then add the desired toppings.

● Hot Chocolate

Always check for food sensitivities and allergies before serving food to children.

Materials: cocoa, polystyrene cups, water, popsicle sticks or coffee stirrers

 This cooking activity should follow the **Marshmallow Math** activity on page 107.

Place two to three teaspoons full of cocoa in each cup. Have a classroom aid or volunteer heat a gallon of water in the microwave. Fill cups $\frac{2}{3}$ full and let children stir and add marshmallows. Yum!

 Follow with the "Hot Chocolate Rap" on page 100 of this theme.

Art/Cooking

Watercolor Mitten Pattern

Math

Snowman Match

Materials: 8 ½" x 11" white and blue construction paper, small bowls, white paint, cotton swabs

For each student, copy the Snowman Match on page 108. Prior to this activity, prepare the background paper for students. Cut three wavy strips, horizontally, on a 8 ½" x 11" sheet of white construction paper. You will need one strip per student. Glue one wavy strip to the bottom of a 8 ½" x 11" blue sheet of construction paper. This will represent the snow.

Model for children how to match the snowman to his correct hat. *First color each snowman's scarf and cut them out. Glue the snowmen on the "snow." The order is irrelevant. Then, look at the scarf of one of the snowman. What pattern is it? What colors did you color it? Find the matching hat and color it with the same colors as the the scarf. Cut it out and glue it on the head of the appropriate snowman. Do the same for the remaining snowmen.* When all of the hats are on, give each table a small bowl of white paint and each child a cotton swab. Instruct them to dip the swab in the paint and then dab it on the blue background to show falling snow. Put the papers in the drying rack to dry and display in your classroom or hallway.

What Comes in Pairs?

 Read the poem "What's a Pair?" on page 99.

Discuss what makes a pair. On chart paper, brainstorm things that come in pairs. Here are some ideas to prompt children if they have difficulty.

shoes/boots	twins	eyes
windshield wipers	iceskates	earrings
socks	skis	bicycle tires
drum sticks	stilts	eyeglass lenses
birds' wings	chopsticks	shoelaces
ice dancers	cymbals	mittens/gloves
legs	hands	feet

Leave the chart available for children to add their ideas throughout the week.

Math

Mittens or Gloves Graph

Copy the Survey Graphic Organizer on page 109. You will need one copy for each child. Explain to children that they are going to take a survey. They are going to survey which of their friends wear mittens and which of their friends wear gloves. You will have children that say they wear both. Tell them to think about what they wore to school that day and to write their name in that column.

Have children take out a pencil and put their name on their own paper. Model for them how you would walk over to a friend and say, *Jayne, do you wear gloves or mittens? Jayne can ask me the same question. She can be signing my graph while I am signing hers.* Stress that children must ask the question to each friend that signs their paper. Children will have five minutes to walk around the classroom and find out which of their friends wear gloves and which wear mittens.

Remind children that you will set the timer. When the timer goes off, they are to return to their seats and tally their results. If you teach tallies as part of your calendar routine, this will be practice for them. If not, you will have to help children tally their results. You may choose to count the results and write the number. You may need to help children with this last step depending on the ability of your students.

Patterning

Invite children to sit in a circle. Distribute plastic interlocking cubes in one or two colors. Review how to create an *ab* pattern. Choose two colors and begin the pattern: red, yellow, red. Ask children, *What comes next?* Repeat with another color. Continue until you feel children can complete a pattern on their own. If they are ready, create an *abc* pattern. Blue, green, yellow, blue, _____, yellow. Ask children, *What color is missing?* Give them several more examples and them let them attempt to make their own *abc* pattern.

 When you feel children have had enough practice, explain the **Watercolor Mittens** activity on page 103 of this theme.

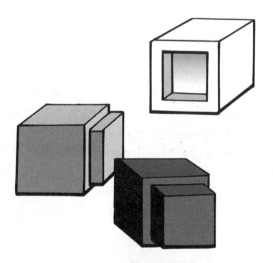

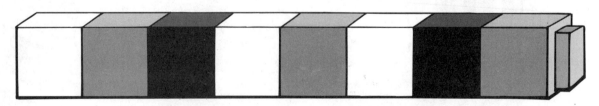

Math

● Marshmallow Math

Always check for food sensitivities and allergies before serving food to children.

Materials: 9" x 12" colored construction paper, small bowls, mini-marshmallows, storyboard picture (page 110)

Prior to this activity you will need to create storyboards found on page 110 of this theme. Copy the mugs of cocoa, color, and cut them out. Glue them onto 9" x 12" sheets of construction paper and laminate.

Provide each table with a small bowl of mini-marshmallows and a storyboard for each child. Remind children of the peanut story problems they did in the Harvest theme and explain that this is a similar activity. Today they will be using marshmallows to solve their story problems. When they are finished with the activity, children can eat the marshmallows.

Instruct children to count out five to ten marshmallows, depending on the age and ability of your students. Have them put the marshmallows on their storyboard but not in the mug. Remind children to listen carefully as you give them problems to solve.

I put two marshmallows in my cup of cocoa. Model for the children putting two marshmallows "in" the cup. *Then I added three more.* Have children add three. *How many total marshmallows are in my cup?* Remind children to touch count each marshmallow as you touch count them together. *If you counted five marshmallows, give yourself a pat on the back.*

Keep adding marshmallows using the same format. Be sure to stress the words *added, total, all together,* and so on. When all the marshmallows are in the cup, it is time to subtract. If you find this is too difficult for your students, simply have them empty their cup and start over.

We all have ten marshmallows in our cup. The cocoa was so hot that three of the marshmallow melted. Take away three of the marshmallows. How many marshmallows do we have left? Let's touch count and see. If you counted seven, pat your tummy and say "yummy." Continue with this format until all of the marshmallows are out of the mug. You can either continue with more addition and subtraction problems, or you can let the children eat the marshmallows!

Math

Snowman Match

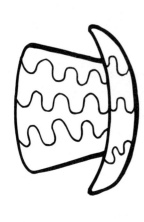

Math

Survey Graphic Organizer

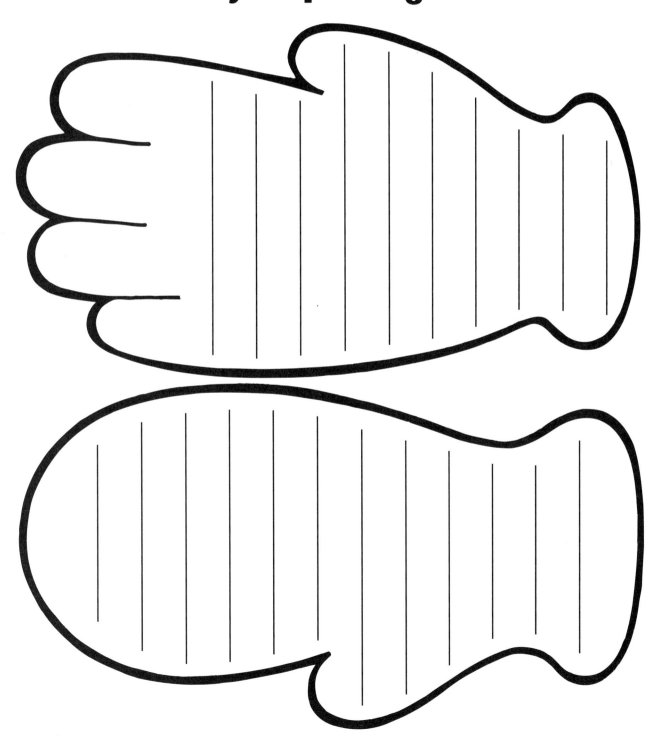

Math

Marshmallow Math Storyboard

Science

Time to Change

Materials: clear plastic cup, ice cubes, items that can be changed such as blocks, building sets, clay, puzzles, paper and markers, or stencils with colored pencils or crayons

Show children a clear plastic cup with several ice cubes inside. *What will happen to this cup of ice if we let it sit on the counter for the rest of the day?* Explain that change is something that happens to us and happens all around us. On chart paper, brainstorm things that change (time, the weather, your age, trees, snow). At each table, put something out that changes when manipulated.

Have children go to their own table. Discuss what is at each table, how it looks, and how it could be changed. Explain that everyone will have an opportunity to create change with each of the items. Give children three minutes at each table. When time has expired, children should stop what they are doing immediately, stand up, and push in their chair. Help children move clockwise to the next table. Once all children are at the correct spot, allow them to continue with the projects that have already been started. Continue until all children end up at their original table. Ask them to share how their projects have changed. *What did it start out as? What is there now? Is there anything that surprised you? If you were at the drawing table, was your picture finished the way you had planned on finishing it? If you were at the building set table, does your creation look the same as when you left? Is it even there?* Show change once more by having children clean up each of their tables.

Telephone

Have children sit in a circle. Ask them to whisper their name to the person sitting next to them. *Was that easy to understand?* Explain that you are going to play a game that may not be so easy. Tell them that you will whisper something to the person sitting on your right. (Try a fairly complex sentence such as *My snowboots have pink and white polka dots and are furry on the inside.*) Then have that person whisper what was said to the person on his or her right and so on all the way around the circle. *When it comes back to me, we will see if the sentence has changed in any way.* Compare what was told to you and what you originally told the person sitting next to you. *Did it change? How much? Where do you think the message started to change? Why?*

Change Experiment

Materials: a small bowl for each table, a clear plastic cup for each child, vinegar, baking soda, tablespoon

Provide each table with a small bowl of vinegar and each child with a clear plastic cup. Go around the room and have children spoon one tablespoon of baking soda into their cup. Have them predict what will happen if they add the vinegar to their cup. Invite them to spoon one tablespoon of vinegar into their cup and to observe what happens. *Did anything change? What changed? What do you think caused the change?* Explain that when the vinegar was added to the baking soda this created a chemical change, and now the two original substances will never be the same again.

Social Studies

● Smiles are Contagious

 Read the poem "Snowgirl" on page 99.

Talk about the last stanza of the poem. *What does it mean, "True smiles never end?" How do you feel when your friend smiles at you? What do you do without even thinking about it when someone smiles at you?*

Smiles are contagious. That means they spread just like germs from a cold can spread. If you sneeze on me, I may catch your germs and get a cold. If you smile at me, then I will probably smile back at you. That is what is meant by saying smiles are contagious. Encourage children to "spread smiles" during their day. When walking in the hallway, playing with their friends, or at home with their family, tell them to spread their smile and see how many smiles they get back.

● How Have You Changed?

At-home activity

See the parent note on page 96. Explain that this is an activity that will need to be done at home and brought back to school by this date (show them on the calendar and count the days). Review the chart-paper poster you created about change. Tell children that they are going to create a pictorial timeline to show how they have changed from birth to their current age. When they bring the timelines back to school, they will have the opportunity to share with the class. You might want to send a short reminder note on the day before timelines are due. If you have a student that forgets to bring their timeline, assure him or her that they can share it with the class on a different day.

Presentation

Invite children to sit in a circle with their pictorial timeline behind them. Go around the circle and have each child share his or her pictures. Encourage them to explain how they have changed physically as well as how their interests, likes, and dislikes have changed. You might choose to share your pictures first to model what is expected of them when it is their turn to share.

● Change the Routine

Change the routine for the day. If you start your day with a story and calendar activity, switch the order. Start with your whole group lesson, centers, or free play. You might choose to create a plan for the day and have children help you write the order in which you will plan your day. Encourage children to share their ideas.

● Class Book

Share the story, *The Snowy Day* by Ezra Jack Keats. Have children brainstorm what they like to do on a snowy day. Record their responses on chart paper. Make a master page containing the following sentence: *On a snowy day I like to_____.* Copy the master page for each student. Invite them to write about their favorite snowy day activity and illustrate their paper. Collect all the pages and create a class book. When reading, allow children to read their page.

Literature Connection

Briggs, Raymond. *The Snowman.* Jefferson City, MO: Scholastic, 1978.

Ehlert, Lois. *Snowballs.* Orlando, FL: Harcourt Brace and Company, 1995.

Keats, Ezra Jack. *The Snowy Day*. Norwalk, CT: Weston Woods Studios, Inc., 1962.

Lweison, Wendy Cheyette. *Hello, Snow!* New York, NY: Grosset and Dunlap, Inc., 1994.

Munsch, Robert. *Thomas' Snowsuit.* Toronto, ON: Annick Press, Ltd., 1985.

Neitzel, Shirley. *The Jacket I Wear in the Snow.* New York, NY: Mulberry Books, 1989.

Schreiber, Anne and Arbo Doughty. *Boots.* Jefferson City, MO: Scholastic, 1994.

Schweninger, Ann. *Wintertime.* Jefferson City, MO: Scholastic, 1990.

Winthrop, Elizabeth. *Sledding.* Jefferson City, MO: Scholastic, 1989.

Polar Animals
Scope and Sequence

	Sound Identification	Letter Identification	Word Study (high frequency words)	Sequencing	Speaking Skills	Listening Skills	Logical Thinking Skills	Social/Emotional Development	Large Motor Development	Fine Motor Movement
Big Book Introduction		●			●	●	●			
Revisiting	●	●	●		●	●	●			
Echo Reading	●	●	●		●	●	●			●
Choral Reading	●	●	●		●	●	●	●		
Partner Reading	●	●	●		●	●	●	●		
Poem: "Copycat"	●	●	●		●	●		●		
Poem: "Slippery Seal"	●	●	●		●	●				
Song: "The Blubber Song"					●	●		●		
Penguin Movement								●	●	
Song: "If I Were…"					●	●	●			
Copycat Motions						●		●	●	
Snowshoes or Skis					●	●		●	●	
Predator or Prey					●	●	●	●	●	
Penguin Art				●	●	●				●
Polar Mural				●	●	●	●			●
Polar Bear Pudding					●	●	●	●		●
Ordinal Numbers				●	●	●	●			●
How Do You Measure ?					●	●	●	●	●	
Adding Odd or Even					●	●	●			●
Geometric Shapes					●	●				●
Blubber or Bare?					●	●		●	●	
Venn Diagram				●	●	●	●		●	
Polar Environment					●	●				
Penguin Rookery					●	●	●	●	●	

Weekly Planner

Skills Practice The letter *Pp* The word *this*	Big Book Little Books Pages 121–122	Poetry/ Skills Page 123	Music and Movement Pages 124–129	Art/Cooking Pages 130–131	Math Pages 132–134	Science Page 135	Social Studies Page 136
Monday	Big Book Introduction: *Polar Animals*	Poem: "Copycat," the letter *Pp* and the word *this*	Song: "The Blubber Song" Copycat		Ordinal Numbers	Blubber or Bare?	Polar Environment
Tuesday	Revisiting: *Polar Animals*	Poem: "Slippery Seal"	Song: "If I Were …" Penquin Movement	Penguin Art	How Do You Measure?		Penguin Rookery
Wednesday	Echo Reading: *Polar Animals*	Little Book: *Polar Animals,* the letter *Pp* and the word *this*	Song and Movement: "Predator or Prey"			Predator or Prey? Venn Diagram	
Thursday	Choral Reading: *Polar Animals*	Little Book: *Polar Animals,* the letter *Pp* and the word *this*	Snowshoes or Skiing	Polar Mural Polar Bear Pudding	Adding Odd or Even		
Friday	Partner Reading: *Polar Animals*			Geometric Snowflakes for the Polar Mural	Geometric Shapes		

Polar Animals

Name: _____

a polar bear

This polar animal has thick wooly fur.

1

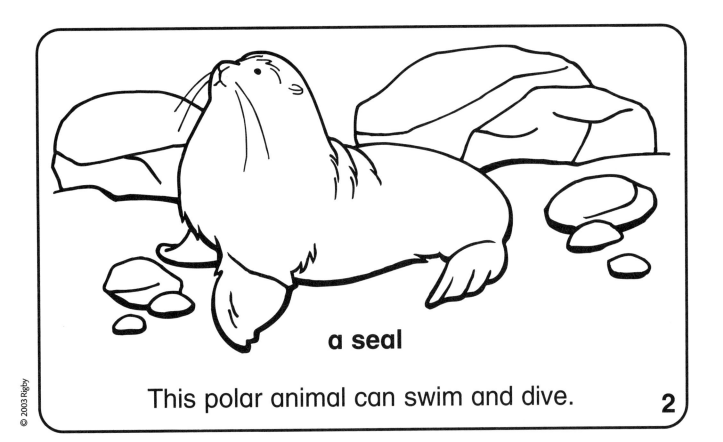

a seal

This polar animal can swim and dive.

2

a grizzly bear

This polar animal sleeps long and deep.

3

a penguin

This polar animal can walk on ice.

an Arctic fox

This polar animal lives in a den.

a lynx

This polar animal can walk on snow.

6

a falcon

This polar animal is the fastest in the world.

7

Date _____

Dear Parents,

Next week we will be beginning a new theme about the amazing animals of the polar regions of the world. We will be learning about the polar bear, seal, grizzly bear, penguin, arctic fox, lynx, and falcon. We will be exploring how these animals survive in their icy habitat including the concepts of predator and prey. You can help reinforce the concepts your child is learning at school by pointing out examples of how animals protect themselves and their babies. In some cases, an animal may try to blend in with its environment. In other cases, it may be able to quickly escape from danger. There are many examples you can cite. You may also want to ask your child to recite any poems or songs they are learning about polar animals.

Thank you for your support.

● Beginning the Theme

Use the Supply Request Letterhead provided on page 11 to hand write a supply request letter. You will want to send supply letters home at least one week before you plan to teach the theme. This will give parents time to send in any materials needed. Please remember to use the Student Materials Record to check off which students brought materials for this theme.

This theme requires the following supplies. Ask parents to help supply:

- **Individually packaged vanilla pudding cups (one for each child)**
- **One or two bags of mini-chocolate chips**
- **Plastic spoons**

Big Book Introduction

● Day One

Prereading

When you create this Big Book, use sticky notes to cover the name of each polar animal.

On a world map, show children where the polar regions are located. Explain that the word arctic refers just to the North Pole and the region around it. In the winter, much of the arctic is covered in snow and ice. In the summer, there is constant daylight. While the summers are lush and warm, the winters are long, cold, and very harsh. Animals from polar regions have certain characteristics that have helped them adapt to their environment. Encourage children to share what they know about these animals and their characteristics. Record their responses on chart paper.

During Reading

As you read the book, use the procedures and questioning techniques presented in the previous units as a guide for sharing this book with the children. After reading the title, turn to the first page and tell children to look at the picture. Encourage them to think back to the chart about polar animals. *Does this look like one of the polar animals we talked about? Which animal do you think it is? What do we already know about this polar animal?* Invite children to share their responses and make a prediction. Using your finger, read the sentence. Ask children if after reading the clue, they want to change their prediction. Lift the sticky note to reveal the name of the polar animal. Point out the letters at the beginning of each polar animal's name. If the animal

was on your chart, circle it in another color. If it was not on the chart, add it and its unique characteristics. Follow the same pattern for the remaining pages.

Post Reading

Now that all of the animals and their names have been revealed, go back and reread the book again. Invite children to lift the flap and read along with you.

Whole Group Reading Strategies

● Day Two

Revisiting: Polar Animals

Revisit the polar animal chart you created yesterday. *Does anyone want to add anything to our polar animal list?* Emphasize the /p/ sound in the word *polar*. *Let's look at the word polar. What sound do you hear at the beginning of the word polar? Find the letter Pp on the front cover of the Big Book. Are there any words on our chart that begin with the same letter/sound as polar? What other words do you know that begin with the same letter/sound as polar?* On chart paper, write the children's suggestions. As you write, use one color for the beginning sound and another for the remaining letters.

Now let's look at the word this. Write the word on the board emphasizing the letters as you write them. Say the word and point to the letters as you read. Tell children that as you are reading, you want them to listen for the word *this*. When they hear it or see it, children can put their thumbs up. Revisit the story and frame the word *this* as you read it. Be sure to use your finger or pointer to indicate one-to-one correspondence.

● Day Three

Echo Reading: Polar Animals

Give children their Little Books to color. Distribute sticky notes to children and model for them how to make the flap for the hidden word. Have children follow along in their Little Books as they echo you. Encourage them to use their finger to match the written word to the spoken word. After reading, revisit the letter/sound *Pp*.

As children echo you, invite them to use their favorite color to underline the word *this* and circle the

letter *Pp*. Follow the same procedure for the remaining pages. Collect the books for Days Four and Five.

● Day Four

Choral Reading: Polar Animals

Distribute the Little Books and read aloud together. Encourage children to use their finger as they read. Watch for left-to-right progression. Focus on the letter/word *Pp* and the word *this*. Collect books for Day Five.

● Day Five

Partner Reading: Polar Animals

As children read together, use the checklist on page 184 or make anecdotal notes about student's concepts about print skills. See Marie Clay's *An Observation Survey of Early Literacy Achievement* for a complete listing of print skills.

Key Vocabulary

Introduce these words throughout the week. Engage children in discussions about the words. When appropriate provide tangible examples to illustrate the meaning of each word. Use the vocabulary word cards found on page 182 to reinforce the words.

hibernate	blubber
camouflage	rookery
climate	snowshoes

Poetry

 Follow the movements on page 125 that correspond to the following poem.

Copy the following poem on chart paper. After reading, invite children to frame the letter *Ss*. Review the sound *Ss* makes. If you have the word *see* on your word wall, you might choose to point out the difference between the two words *see* and *sea*. Clarify that although they sound the same, they are spelled differently and have different meanings.

Copycat

Run like a polar bear,

Waddle like a penguin.

Bark like a seal,

Fly like a falcon.

Creep like a fox.

Walk like a lynx.

It's fun to copy polar animals,

Don't you think?

Slippery Seal

One slippery seal

Who is as hungry as can be,

Spied a shrimp swimming in the sea.

The shrimp told the seal,
"You can't catch me!"

And they swam, and they swam
in the deep blue sea.

Music and Movement

The Blubber Song

(Sung to the tune of "Pop Goes the Weasel")

All around the icy North Pole

The animals roam and play.

They have blubber to help
keep them warm,

All night and day.

● Penguin Movement

Have children stand with their hands at their sides.
Place heels together with toes pointing out.
Encourage children to waddle about the classroom.

 See the **Penguin Rookery** lesson on
page 136 that accompanies this large
motor activity.

If I Were . . .

*(Sung to the tune of
"Do You Know the Muffin Man?")*

If I were a polar bear,
A polar bear, a polar bear,
If I were a polar bear,
I'd run on snow and ice.

If I were a slippery seal,
A slippery seal, a slippery seal,
If I were a slippery seal,
I'd swim and play all day.

If I were a sleek penguin,
A sleek penguin, a sleek penguin,
If I were a sleek penguin,
I'd waddle to and fro.

If I were a great-horned owl,
A great-horned owl, a great horned-owl,
If I were a great-horned owl,
I'd screech and hoot all night.

If I were a beluga whale,
Beluga whale, beluga whale,
If I were a beluga whale,
I'd have great strength and might.

Music and Movement

Write the "Copycat" poem on chart paper and model the following movements.

Copycat Motions

Run like a polar bear,	*Run in place.*
Waddle like a penguin	*Waddle back and forth with your arms at your sides and your hands pointing out.*
Bark like a seal.	*Clap your hands down in front of you and make a barking noise.*
Fly like a flacon.	*Spread your arms wide and sway back and forth.*
Creep like a fox	*Stand on tiptoe with your hands curled by your face and tiptoe in place.*
Walk like a lynx	*Spread your fingers wide like big paws and put one in front of the other out in front of you.*
It's fun to copy polar animals.	*Stretch arms up over your head with fingers wide.*
Don't you think?	*Bend elbows and put hands on either side of your head like you are asking a question.*

● Snowshoes or Skis

You might choose to have this activity accompany the **Odd or Even** math lesson on page 132.

Explain the difference between snowshoes and cross-country skis. If possible, bring in a pair of each to share. Talk about how polar animals have natural characteristics that help them walk on snow and ice (penguins slide on their belly; the lynx has big, wide paws; moose have heavy hooves;), but humans need a little help.

Model for children how to walk in snowshoes and in skis. *With snowshoes, lift your leg high and take a giant step. Rest your foot gently on the snow so you don't sink deep. For cross-country skis alternate arms and legs in a swinging motion as you glide effortlessly around the classroom.*

On scraps of paper, write the numbers one through ten and repeat as needed to ensure each student will get a number. Depending on your students' ability, you might choose to write the total number of students in your class. Either way, each child will take a number out of the bucket. Assign odd numbers to snowshoes and even numbers snow skis. If children aren't sure whether their number is odd or even, have plastic-colored cubes on hand for them to create a number tower to determine if their number is odd or even. Remind them that if every cube has a partner, it is an even number, if there is a cube without a partner, it is an odd number. Allow children to *step* and *ski* around the classroom. Return to the circle and have a few children share their numbers. Using plastic-colored cubes, review how to differentiate between odd and even.

Music and Movement

 Use the "Predator or Prey" song to introduce this activity.

Predator or Prey

(Sung to the tune of "There's a Hole in the Bucket")

There are predators in the arctic,
the arctic, the arctic.

There are predators in the arctic
that hunt for their prey.

The predators are bigger and stronger
and faster.

The predators catch prey that
cannot get away.

● Predator or Prey

Enlarge the polar animal pictures on pages 127–129 and copy enough for each child. Ensure a balance of predators and prey. Color, cut, and laminate for durability. Tape an animal to each child's back. Tell the predators what animal they are wearing. Once everyone is "wearing" an animal, allow children to walk around the room looking for their prey. If a child is caught by a predator, he or she will look at the predator's picture. Knowing the predator should give the child a clue about what type of animal he or she is wearing. The child has three chances to guess the animal on his or her back before the predator moves on for another hunt. Tell children that they cannot catch two animals that are already talking. Tell children they must wait or move on to another animal that is wandering alone.

When they think they know what their animal is, they are to come to you and tell you. When all children have identified their animal correctly come back to the circle. Have them put their animal picture on their chest. Go around the circle and have each child share their animal name and if they are a predator, prey, or both. Play the game again having children switch animal tags. If it is a nice day, this is a great outdoor game.

 See the **Predator or Prey** science activity on page 135 that accompanies this game.

Music and Movement

Predator or Prey Animals

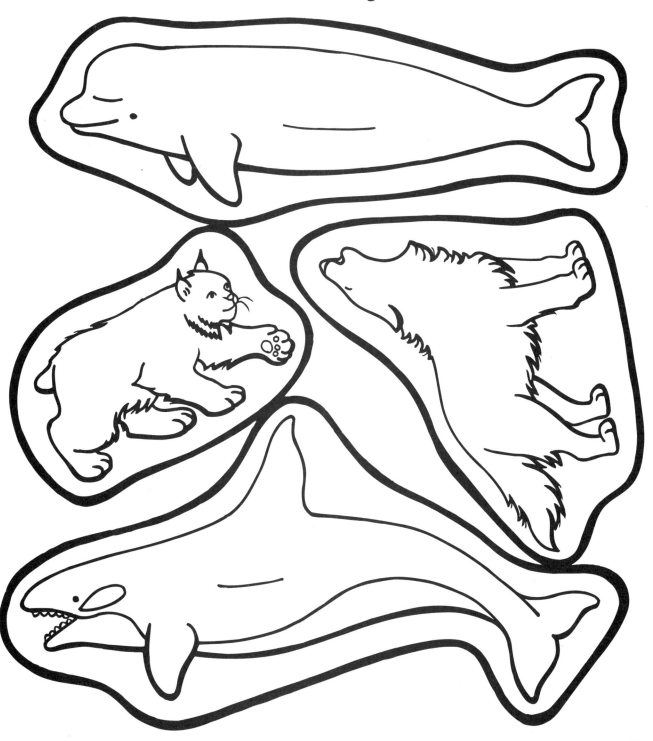

Music and Movement

Predator or Prey Animals

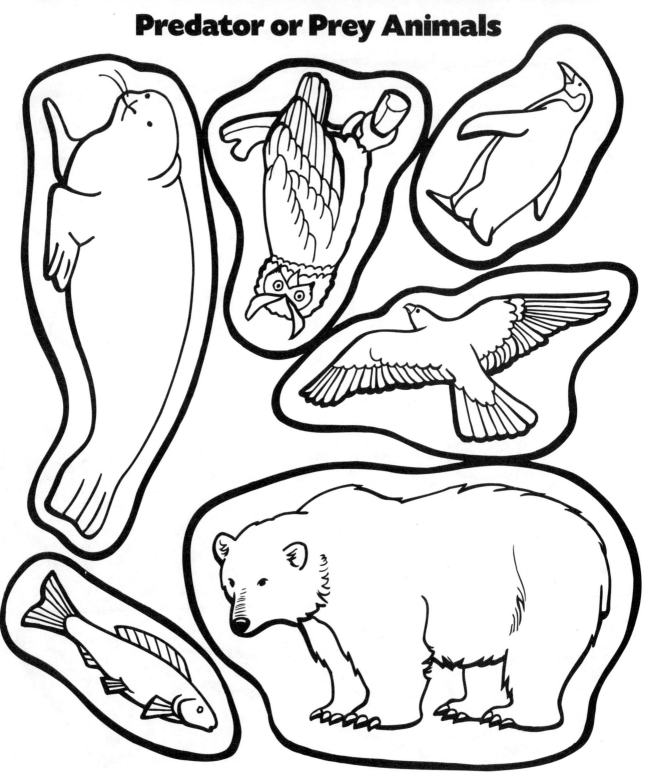

Music and Movement

Predator or Prey Animals

Art/Cooking

● Penguin Art

Materials: 12" x 18" black construction paper, 9" x 12" white construction paper, 5" x 5" squares of orange construction paper, crayons, scissors, and glue

Make templates (one template per group) for the penguin body.

Create cardboard templates of the penguin body for children to trace and cut out. Have them trace the shape onto black paper and write their name on the back using a white crayon. Prepare ahead of time the white oval belly, orange feet, and small white eyes. Once the body has been cut and children have all the other pieces, model for them how to put the penguin together. Explain that the top of the penguin is big and wide. Fold the top in half length-wise and cut a diagonal slit to create the penguin nose. With a black crayon add black dots to the small white circles to form the eyes. Glue the eyes on both sides of the nose. Glue the oval shape on the belly. Finally, fold the top edge of the foot to create an edge and glue it to the bottom of the penguin. The fold will make it look as if the foot is parallel to the ground. Place the penguins in the drying rack. Later display them in the hall or in your classroom.

● Polar Mural

Use this activity with the **Geometric Shapes** math lesson on page 133.

Prepare ahead of time 5-inch circles cut from blue construction paper, copies of the geometric shapes on page 134, enlarged copies of the polar animals on page 127–129, and a large sheet of white butcher paper.

On the butcher paper, draw polar ice caps and floating icebergs. Have children use crayons and markers to color the polar animals and cut them out. Invite them to glue the animals onto the mural.

Distribute copies of the geometric shapes on page 134. Review the qualities and names of the shapes: square, triangle, rhombus, trapezoid, pentagon, and hexagon. Send home a copy of the blackline master with each child and ask parents to help cut out the geometric shapes. Children should return the shapes in a sealed plastic baggie. On the blue circles, have children place the geometric shapes to create snowflakes for the mural. Have children glue the snowflakes to the mural. Display the polar scene in your classroom or hallway.

Art/Cooking

● Polar Bear Pudding

Always check for food sensitivities and allergies before serving food to children.

Materials: vanilla pudding cups, mini-chocolate chips, plastic spoons

Review what children know about polar bears and list their ideas on chart paper. Ask if they know what the word *camouflage* means. Tell them to think about the polar bear. *Why is it white? Why isn't it brown or black like a grizzly bear?* Help children to understand that the white fur of the polar bear helps it to camouflage itself or blend in while it is hunting for its prey (mainly the arctic fox, seal, and walrus). *What distinguishing feature of the polar bear would you be able to see? What stands out from the white?* Their big, black nose!

On each table place a small bowl of mini-chocolate chips. Give each child a vanilla pudding cup and a spoon. Have them add one teaspoon of mini-chocolate chips into their pudding. Mix it up and ask them how hard or easy it is to see the chips. Have children imagine they are in the arctic, and all they see for miles around is white landscape, but occasionally, they see a black dot. Could it be a polar bear nose they spy?

Divide the remainder of the chocolate chips equally among the children's pudding cups.

Math

● Ordinal Numbers

Materials: photocopies of the polar animals on pages 127–129

Invite children to sit in a circle. Choose one child to stand in the middle, then choose another child. *Katherine was the first person I chose, and James was the second.* Continue to add children and count off using ordinal numbers. Count as high as you feel your students are able to comprehend.

For independent practice, shrink the pictures of the polar animals on pages 127–129 to fit on one page. Copy one page for each child in the class. Have children color and cut out the animals. Have them listen as you call out the names of the animals. Tell children to put the animals in the correct order. Then ask them which animal is first, second, and so on. For example you might say:

The penguin is first; the polar bear is second; the fox is third; the seal is fourth; and the lynx is fifth. To get children to say the ordinal numbers back to you, say, *Which one is the fox? Which one is the penguin? Which one is the seal? Which one is the lynx? Which one is the polar bear?* Or you could say, *Is the fox first, second third, fourth, or fifth?*

Rearrange the order and continue practicing as many times as needed.

● How Do You Measure?

Materials: butcher paper, markers, tape or staples

The largest of all penguins is the emperor penguin. At three and a half feet and over sixty pounds, these hefty birds are about the same size as most of the children in your class. On butcher paper, draw an outline of the emperor penguin. Place the outline with the feet of the penguin on the floor and tape it to the wall. Invite children to compare their size to that of the emperor penguin. Write the child's name at the point where the top of his or her head hits the outline. Children can see how they compare.

● Adding Odd or Even

Materials: plastic interlocking cubes

Invite children to sit in a circle. Using plastic-colored cubes, create a tower. Together count the number of cubes in the tower. Show children how to "partner-up" the cubes. If every cube has a partner, then it is an even number. If there is a cube that does not have a partner, it is an odd number. Model this several times before giving children cubes of their own.

Start slow. Have children build a tower of one. *Does it have a partner? Is it odd or even?* Build a tower of two. *Does each cube have a partner? Is it odd or even?* Continue until you have built a tower of ten. Help children to see the pattern: odd, even, odd, even, and so on. Then have children break down their towers and repeat the activity, this time mixing up the order of the numbers.

 Follow this activity with the **Snowshoes or Skis** movement activity on page 125.

Math

● Geometric Shapes

Materials: one set of tangrams

Using tangram pieces, name each shape and explain their qualities.

Triangle-A triangle has three sides. Sometimes all of the sides are equal, sometimes only two sides are equal, and sometimes all of the sides are different lengths.

Rectangle–A rectangle has two equal short sides and two equal long sides.

Square–A square has four sides that are all the same length.

Rhombus–A rhombus has four sides of equal length and opposite sides are parallel.

Trapezoid–A trapezoid has four sides with one pair of parallel sides.

Pentagon–A pentagon has five sides.

Hexagon–A hexagon has six sides.

Put one of each shape in an opaque bag. Invite children to sit in a circle. Explain that you will come around to each of them and tell them the name of a shape. Children will need to use their sense of touch to find the shape in the bag. If they can't remember the qualities of the shape, encourage their classmates to help them out.

Use this lesson before creating the snowflakes for the **Polar Mural** on page 130. Use the blackline master on page 134 to create giant snowflakes that can be added to the mural.

Math

Geometric Shapes

Please cut out each shape and return the pieces in a sealed plastic baggie on_____.

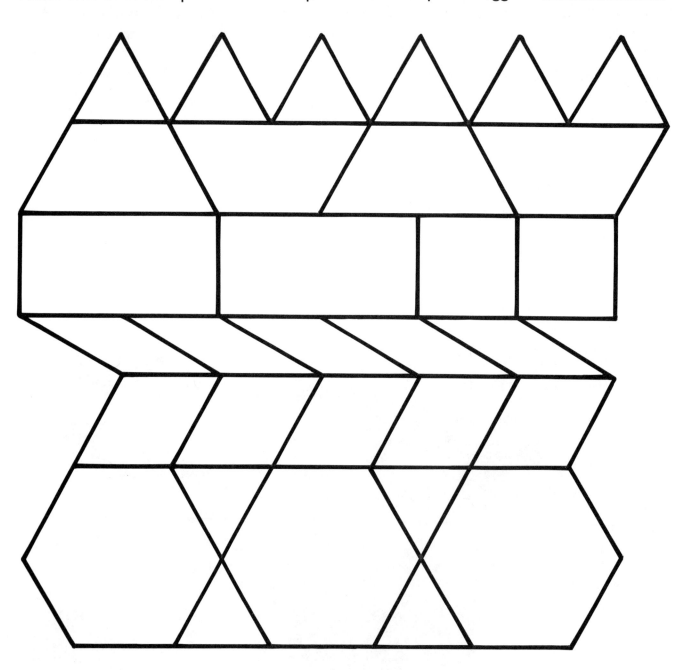

Science

Blubber or Bare, Which Would You Wear?

Materials: two plastic bowls, ice cubes, solid vegetable shortening, spoon, zipper bag

Explain to children that many polar animals have a thick layer of blubber that helps to protect them from the cold arctic environment. To provide a tangible example, fill two plastic bowls with ice. Place a cup of solid vegetable shortening in a zipper bag. Put the zipper bag with the vegetable shortening in it on top of one of the bowls of ice. Invite children to put their hands on each of the bowls of ice. Have them explain the difference between the bare hand that is on the ice and the hand that has a layer of blubber between it and the ice. *Which hand can stay on the ice longer?*

Predator or Prey Venn Diagram

Materials: polar animals pages 127–129, sentence strips, markers, glue, masking tape

Copy, color, and cut out the polar animals on pages 127–129. Write the names of the polar animals on sentence strips and glue the matching picture to it. Create masking tape circles on the floor or use hoola hoops to make a large Venn Diagram. Above each circle on a sentence strip write *Predator* and *Prey*. Write *Both* on a label for the overlap of the circle.

Together talk about the animals and their characteristics: size, strength, speed, and so on. Help children sort the animals into the correct category.

Fish are prey to penguins.

A penguin is prey to seals and whales.

A moose is prey to wolves and bears.

The great horned owl is prey to a lynx and wolverine.

The falcon's eggs are prey to foxes and owls.

The arctic fox is prey to polar bears.

Reindeer are prey to wolves and bears.

Polar bears are prey to killer whales and walrus herds.

A seal is prey to a polar bear.

A walrus is prey to polar bears and killer whales.

A beluga whale is prey to polar bears and killer whales.

 Follow with the **Predator or Prey** game on page 126.

Social Studies

● Polar Environment

Materials: map of the United States

On a map of the U.S.A., locate the state in which you live. Talk about its climate and compare it to other regions north, south, east, or west of you. Explain to children that just like our nation has different regions, so does Antarctica. Antarctica is divided into three regions: the polar ice caps, the tundra, and the taiga. The *polar sea* is covered with frozen ice caps. The area surrounding the sea is called the *tundra*. There is actually little snow in the tundra. The tundra is a flat, extremely windy, treeless region. Beyond the tundra is the *taiga*. The taiga consists of an enormous evergreen forest. All three regions have found a way to survive and support life through the long, cold, harsh winters and flourish in the constant daylight of the midnight sun.

● Penguin Rookery

Penguins live together in large groups called *rookeries*. Penguin families are very close and can distinguish their family members from other penguins by the sounds they make. Divide the class into penguin families of four. Have each penguin family decide on a sound that will distinguish them from other penguins (*eek, aak, ick, ike, awk*). Have each group share their sound. Then have children use their best penguin waddle to move around the classroom, away from their family. Tell children that when you give the signal, they will find their family members. Each penguin will make their family sound until the members of the family have reunited. Once all groups are back together, explain that this is how parents find their babies after they have been out hunting for food.

Use the **Penguin Movement** activity on page 124.

Literature Connection

Asch, Frank. **Song of the North.** Orlando, FL: Gulliver Books, 1999.

Baker, Alan. **The Arctic (Look Who Lives In).** New York, NY: Peter Bedrick Books, 1999.

Butterfield, Moira. **Animals in Cold Places (Looking At).** Orlando, FL: Raintree/SteckVaughn, 1999.

Gallop, Louise. **Owl's Secret (Last Wilderness Adventure).** Homer, AK: Paws IV, 1994.

de Beer, Hans. **Little Polar Bear.** New York, NY: North-South Books, Inc., 1994.

Himmelman, John. **Pipaluk and the Whales.** Washington, District of Columbia: National Geographic Society, 2002.

London, Jonathan. **Ice Bear and Little Fox.** Myrtle Beach, SC: Dutton Books, 1999.

Main, Katy. **Baby Animals of the North.** Seattle, WA: Alaska Northwest Books, 1992.

Wadsworth, Ginger. **Tundra Discoveries.** Watertown, MA: Charlesbridge, 1999.

Yolen, Jane. **Welcome to the Ice House.** Jefferson City, MO: Scholastic, 1998.

Nutrition
Scope and Sequence

	Sound Identification	Letter Identification	Word Study (high frequency words)	Sequencing	Speaking Skills	Listening Skills	Logical Thinking Skills	Social /Emotional Development	Large Motor Development	Fine Motor Movement
Big Book Introduction					●	●	●			
Revisiting			●		●	●	●			
Echo Reading	●	●	●		●	●	●			
Choral Reading	●	●	●		●	●	●			
Partner Reading	●	●	●		●	●	●	●		
Poem: "Food Pyramid"	●	●	●		●	●	●		●	
Poem: "Ice Cream"	●	●	●		●	●				
Song: "Strong and Healthy"					●	●				
Song: "Food Group"					●	●	●			
High/Low Energy Foods					●	●	●	●	●	
Food Pyramid Placemats				●	●	●	●	●		●
Shake It Up!				●	●	●		●		●
Lunch Celebrations					●	●		●		
Oat Ring Math					●	●	●			●
Food Pattern Headbands				●	●	●	●	●		●
Egg Carton Counting					●	●	●	●		●
From the Ground or From a Tree?					●	●	●	●		
From Farm to You				●	●	●	●			●
Floor Food Pyramid					●	●	●	●	●	
Food Group Posters					●	●	●	●	●	
Plan a Healthy Meal					●	●	●	●		●

Weekly Planner

Skills Practice The letter *Nn* The word *and*	Big Book/ Little Books Pages 144–145	Poetry/ Skills Page 146	Music and Movement Pages 147–148	Art/Cooking Pages 149–151	Math Pages 152–155	Science Pages 156-157	Social Studies Page 158
Monday	Big Book Introduction: *The Food Pyramid*	Poem: "Food Pyramid"	Song: "Strong and Healthy"		Oat Ring Math		Floor Food Pyramid
Tuesday	Revisiting: *The Food Pyramid*	Little Book: *The Food Pyramid,* the word *and* and the letter *Nn*		Food Pyramid Placemat	Food Pattern Headband	From the Ground or From a Tree?	
Wednesday	Echo Reading: *The Food Pyramid*	Poem: "Ice Cream," the word *and* and the letter *Nn*	Song: "Food Group"	Shake It Up!		From Farm to You	Food Group Posters
Thursday	Choral Reading: *The Food Pyramid*	Little Book: *The Food Pyramid*			Egg Carton Counting (one dozen)		Plan a Healthy Meal
Friday	Partner Reading: *The Food Pyramid*		High/Low Energy Foods	Healthy Lunch Celebration			

The Food Pyramid

Name:_____

bread, cereal, rice, and pasta

1

fruits and vegetables

2

milk and cheese

3

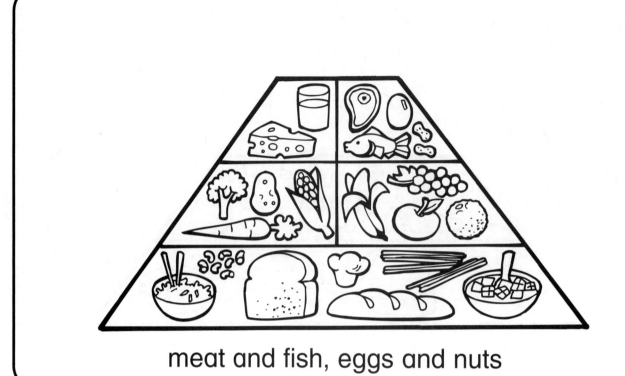

meat and fish, eggs and nuts

4

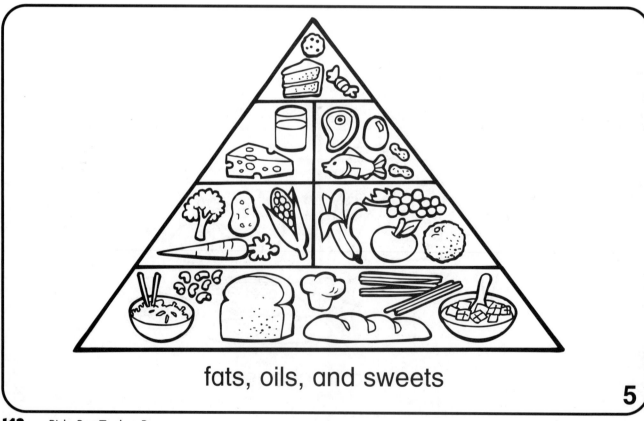

fats, oils, and sweets

5

Date _____

Dear Parents,

In today's fast-paced world, eating healthy is more difficult than ever. Next week, we will begin our new theme—Nutrition. We will explore food groups, exercise, and making healthy choices. You can help reinforce the concepts we are learning in class by pointing out the food groups represented in your child's meals. You can provide your child with healthy snack choices. Ask your child to tell you about the nutrition poems and songs that he or she is learning in school.

As a culminating activity to our nutrition theme, we are planning a healthy lunch day. On _____, please have your child bring their lunch to school in a paper bag. Included in their lunch should be a food from each of the five food groups. Allow your child to help plan their lunch. Have them share what they think would create a balanced meal. We will be eating lunch during our regular session. Milk will be provided at school. Please alert me to any food allergies your child may have.

Thank you for your cooperation.

● Beginning the Theme

Use the Supply Request Letterhead provided on page 11 to hand write a supply request letter. You will want to send supply letters home at least one week before you plan to teach the theme. This will give parents time to send in any materials needed. Please remember to use the Student Materials Record to check off which students brought materials for this theme. This theme requires the following supplies. Ask parents to help supply:

- empty food containers with nutrition labels
- 2 gallons whole milk
- 3 cups sugar
- 1 bottle vanilla extract
- 3 bags of ice
- zipper bags–large and small, enough of each size for each child in your class
- 1 container table salt
- 2 boxes oat ring cereal
- egg cartons (empty), one for each child

Big Book Introduction

● Day One

Prereading

 Use the **Floor Food Pyramid** activity on page 158 to help build background knowledge for this book.

Begin the theme by asking children to share what they know about the food pyramid.

Invite children to sit around the Floor Food Pyramid you have created. (See page 158.) Place one of the empty food cartons you have collected in each of the food groups on the pyramid. After listening to children share what they know, explain to them that we follow the rules of the food pyramid to make sure we eat a healthy, balanced diet. You might need to clarify that diet has two meanings, but both meanings involve keeping track of what you are eating to include healthy, nutritious choices.

During Reading

Show the front cover of the Big Book and review each of the food groups. Revisit the high-frequency word *the*. Talk about the shape of the pyramid and how it gets smaller as it goes up. Ask children to share why they think this is so. Help them to understand that the base of the pyramid, the bread and cereal/rice and pasta, is the largest food group. We eat more servings from this group every day than any other group. Compare the size of the remaining groups to each other as well as the bread and cereal group. Using a pointer,

read the title of the book aloud. As you read to the children, stress the high-frequency word *and*. Invite children to read that word with you as you point to the words. After reading each page, point out how the pyramid is continuing to grow as you read about each group.

Post Reading

Be sure to read the story again without stopping or asking questions. Invite children to read along with you if they choose. Continue pointing to the words as you read. For the remaining days, follow the Whole Group Reading Strategies.

Whole Group Reading Strategies

● Day Two

Revisiting: The Food Pyramid

Have children recall the five food groups. On the first page of the Big Book, frame the word *and*. Introduce and write the word *and* on the board, emphasizing the letters as you write them. Add *and* to your word wall. Now frame the letter *Nn* in the Big Book and ask children to point to the letter in their Little Books. Invite children to repeat you as you say the letter name and sound. Encourage them to think of words that contain the letter/sound *Nn*. Write the words on chart paper. Be sure to use two different colored markers. One for the /n/ sound and another for the other letters. Tell children that you are going to read the story to them and they can listen and/or read along. Be sure to use your finger or a pointer as you read. After reading, give children their Little Books and allow them to color the pictures. Reread it together and have them circle the high-frequency word *and*. Collect the books for Days Three, Four, and Five.

● Day Three

Echo Reading: The Food Pyramid

Have children follow along in their Little Books as they echo you. Encourage them to use their finger to match the written word to the spoken word as they are reading. After reading, frame the word *and* on each page of the Big Book. Have children point to the word in their Little Books. Review the letter/sound *Nn*. Ask children to think of names that begin with the letter *Nn*. This will allow them to practice recognition of the uppercase letter *N*. Add the names to your list of words containing the letter *Nn*. Collect the books for Days Four and Five.

● Day Four

Choral Reading: The Food Pyramid

Distribute the Little Books and read aloud together. Encourage children to point to each word as they read it. Focus on the high-frequency word *and*. Help children read it on each page. Watch for the left-to-right progression. After choral reading, have children return to their seats and write in the number of daily servings needed for each food group. Depending on the age level and ability of your students, you might need to write the numbers on the board or help them write the numbers on each page. Revisit the book page by page. Collect the books for Day Five.

● Day Five

Partner Reading: The Food Pyramid

As children read together, use the checklist on page 184 or make anecdotal notes about students' individual concepts about print skills. See Marie Clay's *An Observation Survey of Early Literacy Achievement* for a complete listing of print skills.

Key Vocabulary

Introduce these words throughout the week. Engage children in discussions about the words. When appropriate provide tangible examples to illustrate the meaning of each word. Use the vocabulary word cards found on page 183 to reinforce the words.

healthy	diet
dairy	protein
pyramid	dozen

Poetry

After reading the Big Book, divide the remainder of the empty food containers onto the Floor Food Pyramid. Read aloud the following poem and have children pick out foods that would complete the servings they would need for the day. Be sure to mention that the container tells you how much one serving size is. For example, if a person chooses oat rings cereal for a bread group, they don't have to eat the whole box. Tell children that the container says one cup of oat rings equals one serving. You may want to show children what one cup of oat rings looks like. This provides an excellent visual representation of what they should be including in their healthy diet. Focus on the letter/sound /Nn/ and the high-frequency word *and*.

Food Pyramid

A healthy diet means you need
To watch the foods on which you feed.
Follow the pyramid
And do not stray.
Let's count the servings you need each day.
6 to 11 servings of bread, pasta, and rice,
3 to 5 servings of vegetables are nice.
2 to 4 servings of healthy, fresh fruit,
2 to 3 servings from the milk and
    cheese group.
Don't stop now! You still need to eat,
2 to 3 servings of fish, poultry, or meat.
Follow the pyramid, and you will see,
How strong and healthy you can be!

 Use this poem in conjunction with the **From Farm to You** activity on page 156.

Ice Cream

Ice cream is a dairy treat,
That's really very fun to eat.
Listen closely to learn how
This frozen treat starts with the cow.

A cow is milked twice everyday,
After grazing on wheat and hay.
The milk is churned to make ice cream,
Chocolate, vanilla, and strawberry supreme!
The ice cream is taken to the store,
Where parents go when you need more.
They bring the ice cream home to eat,
So grab a spoon and take a seat.
Enjoy a scoop of this dairy treat!

Music and Movement

Strong and Healthy
(Sung to the tune of "Alouette")

To stay healthy, I always watch my diet,
The food pyramid helps show me the way.

I eat bread, rice, cereal, or pasta
As part of my healthy diet everyday.

Fruits and veggies have lots of healthy vitamins.
Vitamins keep germs and colds away.

Milk and cheese have calcium for strong bones.
You need strong bones when you go to play.

Meat and fish are full of needed protein.
You need protein to live and grow each day.

Sweets and treats are yummy, but be cautious.
You should only eat them once a day.

● High/Low Energy Foods

Talk with children about the difference between high energy foods and low energy foods. High energy foods are healthy foods that provide energy for a long duration. Low energy foods provide a quick burst of energy, but over time make you feel more sluggish and tired.

Read the following list of foods. Ask children to run in place to represent a high-energy food. To represent a low-energy food, encourage them to move their arms and legs very slowly.

oatmeal
bananas
candy bar
peanuts
crackers
apple
soda pop
candy
grapes
cheese
orange juice
cookie
cereal bar
cottage cheese
milk
yogurt
doughnut
rice
marshmallows

Music and Movement

Food Group
(Sung to the tune of "Goodnight Ladies")

I like cereal,
  for my breakfast.
Can you tell me,
  In which food group it belongs?

I like carrots,
  they are crunchy.
Can you tell me,
  In which food group they belong?

I like green grapes,
  found in bunches.
Can you tell me,
  In which food group they belong?

I like yogurt,
  it is creamy.
Can you tell me,
  In which food group it belongs?

I like chicken,
  baked, fried, or broiled.
Can you tell me,
  In which food group it belongs?

I like cupcakes,
  covered with frosting.
Can you tell me,
  In which food group they belong?

I like bagels,
  when they're toasted.
Can you tell me,
  In which food group they belong?

I like green beans,
  from the garden.
Can you tell me,
  In which food group they belong?

I like oranges,
  they are tangy.
Can you tell me,
  In which food group they belong?

I like white milk,
  when it's ice cold.
Can you tell me,
  In which food group it belongs?

I like fish sticks,
  for my dinner.
Can you tell me,
  In which food group they belong?

I like doughnuts,
  loaded with sprinkles.
Can you tell me,
  In which food group they belong?

I like wheat bread,
  on my sandwich.
Can you tell me,
  In which food group it belongs?

I like spinach,
  it makes me strong.
Can you tell me,
  In which food group it belongs?

I like peaches,
  their skin is fuzzy.
Can you tell me,
  In which food group they belong?

I like Swiss cheese,
  on fresh crackers.
Can you tell me,
  In which food group it belongs?

I like burgers,
  cooked on the grill.
Can you tell me,
  In which food group they belong?

I like cookies,
  with chocolate chips.
Can you tell me,
  In which food group they belong?

Art/Cooking

Shake It Up!

Always check for food sensitivities and allergies before serving food to children.

Materials: For each child, you will need one large and one small plastic zipper bag, $\frac{1}{2}$ cup whole milk, one tablespoon sugar, three tablespoons of table salt, one-quarter teaspoon vanilla, about twenty ice cubes, and a plastic spoon.

Use the Supply Request Letterhead on page 11 to request the ingredients needed to make ice cream. Provide each child with one large and one small zipper bag. In the small zipper bag mix the milk, sugar, and vanilla. Seal the bag tightly. You might choose to prepare these ahead of time. In the large zipper bag have children count out about twenty ice-cubes and add the table salt. Have children put the small zipper bag into the large one. Seal the large bag tightly and shake it up. Instruct children to continue shaking their bags until the milk mixture begins to thicken. When it is thick enough to eat, invite them to remove the small bag and dig in!

Food Pyramid Placemat

Materials: Food Pyramid template (see pages 150 and 151), 12" x 18" colored construction paper, scissors, glue

Copy the food pyramid pictures on pages 150–151, one set for each child. Invite children to sit in a circle as you model for them how to make a Food Pyramid placemat. (Children can use the placemat for the healthy lunch celebration.) Color the pictures from each food group and cut the puzzle pieces out. On a piece of 12" x 18" colored construction paper, build the pyramid. Begin by gluing the bread, cereal, rice and pasta group at the bottom, then add the fruits, vegetables, dairy, meats and protein, and finally the sugars and sweets. Remind children to put their name on their placemat and put it in the drying rack. If available, laminate the placemats so after the healthy lunch, children can take them home. They can be used again and again.

Healthy Lunch Celebration

As a culminating activity to the nutrition unit, have children plan a healthy lunch to bring to school on the last day of the unit. See the parent note on page 143. Coordinate details with your cafeteria to provide milk for children.

Art/Cooking

Food Pyramid Template

Art/Cooking

Food Pyramid Template

Math

● Oat Ring Math

Always check for food sensitivities and allergies before serving food to children.

Materials: storyboard (page 153), small bowls, oat ring cereal, plastic spoons.

Use the Supply Request Letterhead on page 11 to request one or two boxes of oat ring cereal. Copy the storyboard on page 153. Provide each table with a small, plastic bowl of oat ring cereal. Invite children to count out ten pieces and put them on their storyboard. Give each child a plastic spoon to drag and count. Revisit the concept of one more and odd and even. Invite children to add one oat ring to their bowl.

Is one an odd or even number? How do you know? What is one plus one more? Add another oat ring to your bowl. If you have two oat rings in your bowl, tap your spoon on the table twice. Is two an even number or an odd number? How do you know? What is two plus one more? Add another oat ring to your bowl.

Continue with the same pattern until all the oat rings are in the bowl. You can then review one less as you remove the oat rings from the bowl. Encourage children to note the *abab* pattern when identifying odd and even numbers. When you are finished counting, invite children to eat the remaining oat rings.

● Egg Carton Counting

Materials: empty egg cartons, cotton balls

Use the Supply Request Letterhead on page 11 to request that every child bring an empty egg carton to school. Put a few handfuls of "eggs" (cotton balls) on each table. Instruct each child to put one egg in each cup. Count the number of eggs in the carton. Explain that a dozen is the same as the number twelve. Give examples of things that come in dozens: eggs, doughnuts, pencils, and so on. Have children take out six eggs from the top row of the egg carton. *How many eggs did you take out? How many eggs are left?* Explain that six is half of a dozen. A half dozen always means six. You can create story problems or review the concept of one more. When the lesson is complete, reinforce the concept of one dozen and a half dozen.

● Food Pattern Headbands

Materials: 15" x 2" strips of construction paper, food pattern pictures (see pages 154–155), crayons, scissors, and glue

Copy the food pattern pictures. Have children cut the pictures out and make an *ab* pattern with the pictures (i.e. apple, fish, apple, fish). Invite a few children to share their patterns. Then have children create an *abc, aab,* and *abb* pattern and share them. Allow them to choose their favorite pattern, color it, and glue it on a 15" x 3" strip of colored construction paper. Remind them that if they chose the apple/fish pattern, they must color all apples identically and all fish identically. Remind children to put their name on the back of the paper strip and lay the finished product in the drying rack. On the day of your healthy lunch celebration, create headbands. Measure the headband to fit the size of the child's head and then fasten it with a staple.

Math

Oat Ring Math Storyboard

Math

Food Pattern Headband

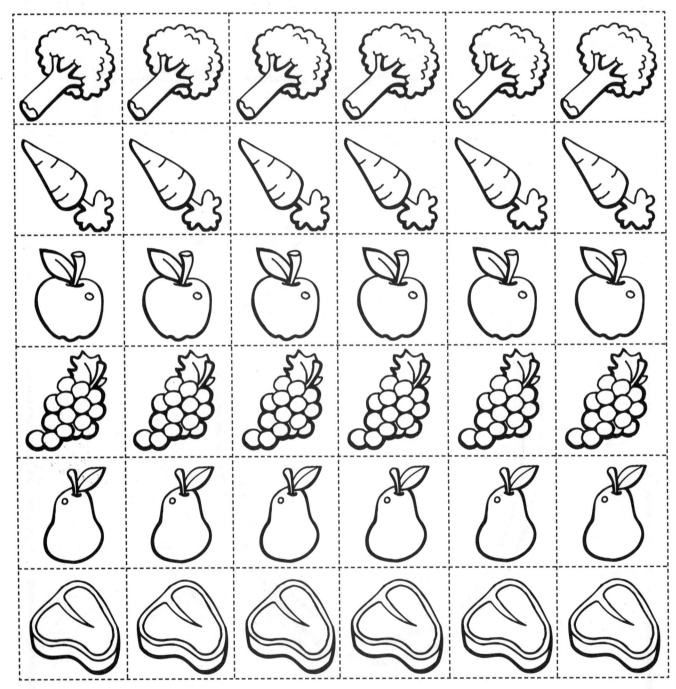

Math

Food Pattern Headband

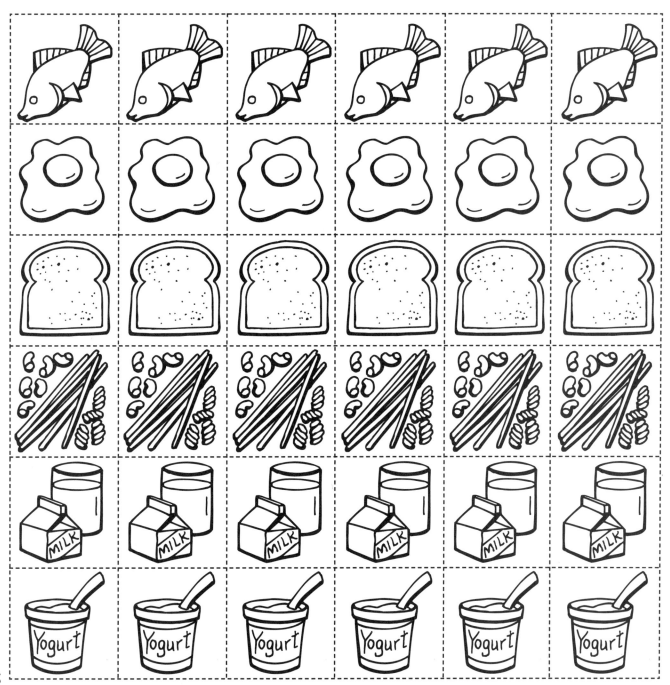

Science

● From the Ground or From a Tree?

Materials: butcher paper, markers

Brainstorm with children types of fruits and vegetables. Write their ideas on chart paper. On a large sheet of butcher paper, draw a rectangle-shaped garden and bare tree. Review the list that you generated as a class. As you name each fruit or vegetable, invite children to draw the fruit or vegetable in the appropriate place where it grows. Help children to label each picture. Display the picture for children to use as a reference throughout the unit.

● From Farm to You

Materials: From Farm to You links, crayons, scissors, glue

 Introduce this activity with the poem "Ice Cream" on page 146.

Photocopy the blackline master of links on page 157 for every child in the class. After reading the poem, create a flow chart on butcher paper or the board to illustrate the process of making ice cream. Discuss with children that some foods must go through many steps before they are ready to eat. In the process, each step must be completed. If one step is missing, the cycle is incomplete. Invite children to sit in a circle. Color the strips and model for children how to cut them out and glue them together to make a From Farm to You chain.

Science

From Farm to You Links

	hay	
	cow	
	milk	
	ice cream	
	store	
	you	

Social Studies

● Floor Food Pyramid

Materials: two-inch wide masking tape, empty food containers

Use the Supply Request Letterhead on page 11 to request empty, clean food containers. Be sure to send this note a week before you plan to teach this unit.

You can use this activity to introduce the Big Book on Day One of reading *The Food Pyramid*. On the floor in your circle area, create a huge food pyramid using two-inch wide masking tape. After reading the Big Book, invite children to put the remainder of the food containers in the appropriate group. Use this as a center activity throughout the week. Have available grocery bags and encourage children to pack a healthy breakfast, lunch, or dinner.

● Food Group Posters

Materials: butcher paper, magazines, scissors, glue

On large, different colored sheets of butcher paper, create a poster for each of the food groups. Write the name of each food group at the top. Instruct children to look through magazines and find a picture for each food group. They should cut out the picture and glue it on the appropriate poster. Remind children to use glue sparingly. You might choose to stand near the posters to ensure that children are pasting them correctly. Display the posters in your classroom for children to use as a reference throughout the theme.

 Use the "Food Groups" song on page 148 in conjunction with this activity.

● Plan a Healthy Meal

Materials: paper plates, magazines, scissors, glue

Tell children that they are going to plan a healthy meal. It can be breakfast, lunch, or dinner, but it must include one item from each of the food groups. Provide each child with a paper plate. Have them write their name on the back. After they choose which meal they are going to plan, instruct them to look through magazines and to find pictures that will complete their healthy meal. Have them paste the pictures on the plate to create a healthy meal. When children are finished, invite them to sit in a circle. Choose a breakfast, lunch, and dinner plate and together, count to see if the three meals would satisfy the daily number of servings needed from each group. Continue until each child has had a chance to share his or her healthy plate.

Literature Connection

Aylesworth, Jim. ***The Burger and the Hot Dog.*** Riverside, NJ: Atheneum, 2001.

Child, Lauren. ***I Will Never Eat a Tomato.*** Cambridge, MA: Candlewick Press, 2000.

Fearnley, Jan. ***Mr. Wolf's Pancakes.*** Waukesha, WI: Little Tiger Press, 2000.

Gray, Kes. ***Eat Your Peas.*** New York, NY: DK Publishing, 2000.

Gustafson, Scott. ***Alphabet Soup: A Feast of Letters.*** Shelton, CN: The Greenwich Workshop Press, 1996.

Hoban, Russell. ***Bread and Jam for Frances.*** New York, NY: HarperCollins Juvenile Books, 1993.

Hoberman, Mary Ann. ***The Seven Silly Eaters.*** Orlando, FL: Browndeer Press, 1997.

Kasza, Keiko. ***The Wolf's Chicken Stew.*** Glenview, IL: Scott Foresman, 1996.

Lauber, Patricia. ***Who Eats What?: Food Chains and Food Webs.*** New York, NY: HarperCollins Juvenile Books, 1995.

London, Jonathon. ***Froggy Eats Out.*** New York, NY: Viking Children's Books, 2001.

Nassau, Elizabeth Sussman. ***The Peanut Butter Jam.*** Santa Fe, NM: Health Press, 2001.

Palatini, Margie. ***Zak's Lunch.*** New York, NY: Clarion Books, 1998.

Rockwell, Lizzy. ***Good Enough to Eat: A Kid's Guide to Food and Nutrition.*** New York, NY: HarperCollins, 1999.

Solheim, James. ***It's Disgusting-And We Ate It!: True Food Facts from Around the World-And Throughout History!*** New York, NY: Simon & Schuster, 1998.

Trumbauer, Lisa. ***Food for Thought.*** Minnetonka, MN: Pebble Books, 2000.

Dental Health

Scope and Sequence

	Sound Identification	Letter Identification	Word Study (high frequency words)	Sequencing	Speaking Skills	Listening Skills	Logical Thinking Skills	Social / Emotional Development	Large Motor Development	Fine Motor Movement
Big Book Introduction	●	●	●		●	●	●	●		
Revisiting	●	●	●		●	●	●			
Echo Reading	●	●	●		●	●	●			
Choral Reading	●	●	●		●	●	●			
Partner Reading	●	●	●		●	●	●	●		
Poem: "Baby Teeth"	●	●	●		●	●	●			
Poem: "Front Teeth"						●				
Song: "Morning and Night"					●	●				
Song: "Loose Tooth"					●	●				
Tooth Puppet				●	●	●	●	●		●
Apple Slice Smiles				●		●	●			●
How Long is a Minute?					●	●	●		●	
Who Is Missing a Tooth?				●	●	●	●	●	●	
Counting by Two's					●	●	●	●		
Why Do We Need to Brush?					●	●	●			
Nature's Toothbrush					●	●	●	●	●	
Parts of the Mouth					●	●	●			
Dental Instruments					●	●	●	●		
Mystery Box					●	●	●	●		●
Visit From a Dentist					●	●		●		

Weekly Planner

Skills Practice The letter *Dd* The word *will*	Big Book/ Little Books Pages 166–167	Poetry/ Skills Pages 168	Music and Movement Page 169	Art/Cooking Page 170	Math Page 171	Science Page 172	Social Studies Page 173
Monday	Big Book Introduction: *The Dentist*		Song: "Morning and Night"			Why Do We Need to Brush?	Parts of the Mouth
Tuesday	Revisiting: *The Dentist*	Little Book: *The Dentist,* the letter *Dd*			Who Is Missing a Tooth?		Dental Instruments
Wednesday	Echo Reading: *The Dentist*	Little Book: *The Dentist,* the word *will* Poem: "Baby Teeth"	Song: "Loose Tooth"	Tooth Puppet			Mystery Box
Thursday	Choral Reading: *The Dentist*	Little Book: *The Dentist,* the letter *Dd* Poem: "Front Teeth"	How Long Is a Minute?		Counting by Two's	Nature's Toothbrush	
Friday	Partner Reading: *The Dentist*			Apple Slice Smile			Visit from a Dentist or Hygienist

The Dentist

Name: _____

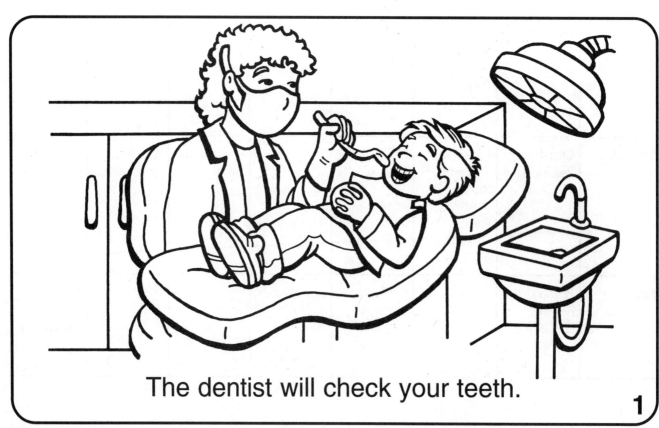

The dentist will check your teeth.

1

The dentist will check your gums.

2

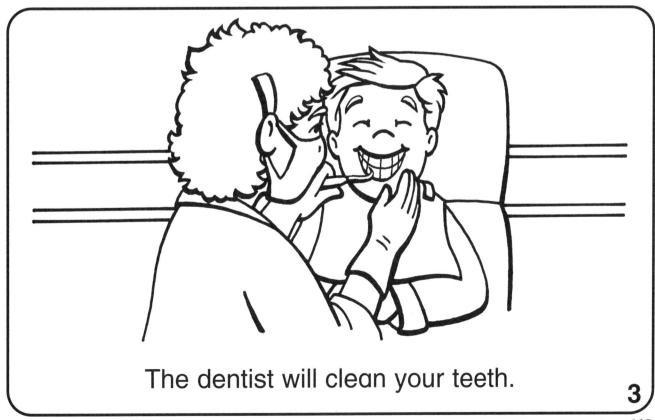

The dentist will clean your teeth.

3

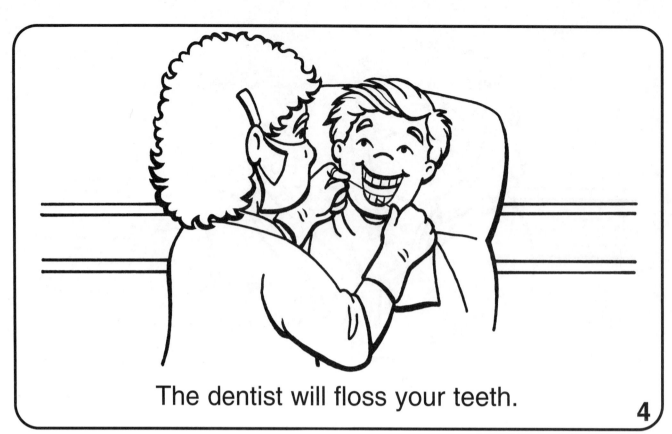

The dentist will floss your teeth.

4

© 2003 Rigby

You will be glad that you went to the dentist!

5

© 2003 Rigby

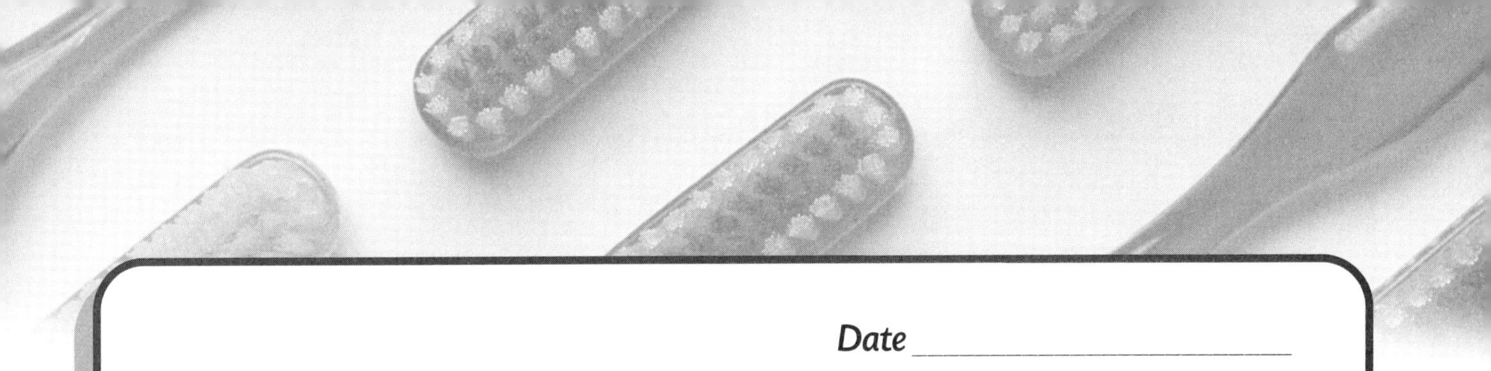

Date _____

Dear Parents,

Next week, we will begin our Dental Health theme. We will be exploring our teeth and gums and how to keep them healthy and clean, and learning about the professionals who care for our teeth and gums. You can help reinforce these concepts at home by pointing out when your child's next dental check up is scheduled, modeling proper brushing and flossing techniques, and limiting tooth decaying sweets. Ask your child to talk to you about the things they are learning in school and to share some of the poems or songs they remember.

Thank you for your support.

● Beginning the Theme

Use the Supply Request Letterhead provided on page 11 to handwrite a request for supplies. You will want to send supply letters home at least one week before you plan to teach the theme. This will give parents time to send in any materials needed. Please remember to use the Student Materials Record to check off which students brought materials for this theme.

This theme requires the following supplies. Ask parents to help supply:

- 3 bags of mini marshmallows
- small paper plates
- 8 large red apples
- 1 eighteen ounce jar creamy peanut butter
- 1 bag small Tootsie Rolls®
- 1 bag baby carrots

Big Book Introduction

● Day One

Prereading

Children will have lots to share about their visits to the dentist. Write their recollections on chart paper. Listen and list what the dentist does, the instruments he or she uses, and any experiences with x-rays or cavities. Invite children to share how they felt before, during, and after the examination. What have they learned from visiting the dentist? Show the front cover of the Big Book and have children explain what each of the instruments does. If they are not sure of their use, ask if they think they will learn what they do by reading the story.

During Reading

Point to the front cover and ask children if there are any words they know. They should recognize the high-frequency word *the*. Have a volunteer frame the word. Read the word *dentist*. Ask children to name the beginning letter and say its sound. Using a pointer, read the title aloud. Invite children to read the high-frequency word *the* with you if they see it again in the story. As you turn to the following page, encourage children to use the picture to help them figure out what is happening. *What is the dentist doing? Do you recognize that dental tool?* Using a pointer, read the sentence aloud and confirm or modify predictions. Follow the same pattern for the remaining pages. Continue to encourage students to use the picture cues to help decode unknown words.

Post Reading

Be sure to read the story again without stopping or asking questions. Invite children to read along with you if they choose. Continue pointing to the words as you read. For the remaining days follow the Whole Group Reading Strategies.

Whole Group Reading Strategies

● Day Two
Revisiting: The Dentist

Have children recall the events in the story. On the first page frame the letter *Dd*. Invite children to brainstorm words that begin with the letter *Dd* and write them on chart paper. Be sure to use two colors, one color
for the beginning sound and another color for the remaining letters. As you read the story, invite children to frame the letter *Dd*. Be sure to use your finger or a pointer as you read. After reading, give children their Little Books and allow them to color the pictures. Reread the story together and have them circle the letter *Dd*. Collect the books for Days Three, Four, and Five.

● Day Three
Echo Reading: The Dentist

Have children follow along in their Little Books as they echo you. Encourage them to use their finger or a pointer to match the written word to the spoken word as they are reading.

After reading, frame the high-frequency word *will* and have children point to it in their Little Books. Reread the story and invite children to circle the word *will* as they read with you. Collect the books for Days Four and Five.

● Day Four
Choral Reading: The Dentist

Distribute the Little Books and read aloud together. Encourage children to point to each word as they read it. Focus on the high-frequency word *will*. Invite volunteers to read aloud independently. Collect the books for Day Five.

● Day Five
Partner Reading: The Dentist

As children read together, use the checklist on page 184 or make anecdotal notes about students individual concepts about print skills. See Marie Clay's *An Observation Survey of Early Literacy Achievement* for a complete listing of print skills.

Key Vocabulary

Introduce these words throughout the week. Engage children in discussions about the words. When appropriate provide tangible examples to illustrate the meaning of each word. Use the vocabulary word cards found on page 183 to reinforce the words.

cavity	fluoride
decay	gums
floss	dentist

Poetry

 Use the following poem to introduce the **Nature's Toothbrush** lesson on page 172.

Help children to understand that the foods we eat can help to prevent or increase tooth decay. Focus on the letter/sound *Dd* and the high-frequency word *will*.

 Use this poem with the **Who's Missing a Tooth** math lesson on page 171.

Materials: butcher paper, markers

After reading this poem, invite children to brainstorm other foods that are difficult to eat without your two front teeth. Write these foods on tooth-shaped butcher paper and display in your classroom.

Baby Teeth

Baby teeth are meant
   to fall out on their own.
Adult teeth will come in
   and last until you're grown.
Be sure to take good care—
   they're the only teeth you've got.
Brush and floss each day
   so your teeth will never rot!

Front Teeth

My two front teeth are missing
   which makes it hard to bite.
I can't eat corn on the cob.
   I've tried with all my might.
I know they'll soon grow in,
   and I'll be able to eat
all those foods I'm missing—
I can't wait for my front teeth!

Music and Movement

Morning and Night

(Sung to the tune of "Camptown Races")

Brush your teeth two times a day
  morning and night.
Doing this will help you keep
  cavities away.
Use a soft toothbrush.
  Brush slowly, don't you rush.
Brush and floss to keep teeth strong.
  Teeth will last your whole life long!

Loose Tooth

(Sung to the tune of "Looby Loo")

(Child's name) had a wiggly tooth
It fell out yesterday
  (or " It just fell out today")
(He/She) now has a special grin
(He'll/She'll) wear till *(his/her)*
  new tooth comes in!

● How Long Is a Minute?

Materials: Clock or watch with second hand

Begin the lesson by explaining to children that when they brush their teeth, they need to brush them for at least two minutes. Ask them to share other things they think might take two minutes to do (make a sandwich, get dressed, walk to school, and so on). Write their responses on chart paper. Explain to children there are sixty seconds in a minute. Mark sixty seconds by swinging a pendulum and having children count time with you. (You can fashion a pendulum by attaching a heavy object to a long rope or string.) After counting, invite children to share if they thought a minute was longer or shorter. Swing the pendulum again to mark time. Have children stand on one foot or jump in place for one minute. Together go through the motions of brushing your teeth, front, sides, top, bottom, reminding children to brush lightly and in small circles. Now have them "brush" their teeth while you time them for two minutes. Invite them to share whether they thought that was a long time. Throughout the remainder of the day use the sixty second time limit to accomplish tasks (clean tables, get a drink, put on your coat) to reinforce the concept.

Art/Cooking

● Tooth Puppet

Materials: small paper plates one for each child, mini-marshmallows, markers, glue

Give children a small paper plate and ask them to fold it in half. Model for children how to draw eyes and a nose on one side of the folded paper plate. On the inside of the "mouth," model how to draw a tongue. Then show children how to glue small marshmallows inside the mouth to represent teeth. Place the tooth puppets in the drying rack. When the puppets are dry, allow students to use the puppets to role-play a visit to the dentist's office.

● Apple Slice Smile

Materials: 8 large red apples, 18 ounce jar of peanut butter, 1 large bag of mini-marshmallows, craft sticks, paper plates

Caution: Peanut product used in this activity.

Cut each apple into eight slices and remove the seeds and core. Give each child two apple slices, a craft stick, six-eight mini-marshmallows, and approximately two tablespoons of peanut butter on a paper plate. Children should use the craft stick to spread peanut butter on one side of each apple slice. Place marshmallows between the two apple slices. You can leave a space between the marshmallows to represent a missing tooth.

Math

● Who Is Missing a Tooth?

Create a people graph by having children divide into two groups, those that have a missing tooth and those that do not. Have children line up parallel to each other and have them make comparisons. *Which group has more/less?* Count each side and write the number for each graph on chart paper. Together create tallies for each number and decide if it is an odd or even number. Remind children to "pair up" to find out if their number is odd or even. Create a Venn Diagram with children by having them divide into those that are missing a tooth, those that are not, and those that have a loose tooth. Use masking tape to create the circles on the floor and have children stand in the appropriate section. Make the same comparisons as before and record the observations on chart paper. Reassure children who have yet to lose a tooth that it won't be long now.

 Use the "Front Teeth" poem on page 168 in conjunction with this activity.

● Counting by Twos

Invite children to smile at their neighbor. Have them count their neighbor's front teeth. If they are missing a tooth remind them that eventually we will all have two front teeth. *Is two an even number or an odd number? Why?* Revisit skip counting by fives and tens. If skip counting is part of your calendar activity, this will be a review. If not, you will want to extend this lesson by using manipulatives to show children how to group numbers in order to count faster. Tell children that just as counting by fives and tens is a fast way to count by grouping numbers, we can also count by twos.

Review odd and even numbers. Tell children that when you count by twos all the numbers are even numbers. Invite three or four children to stand in front of the class. Have them smile big and wide and count their front teeth. Whisper count the odd numbers and in a louder voice say the even numbers. Count them again this time saying only the even numbers. Create a number line on the board and circle the multiples of two. Continue adding children until all are standing. Have them count off by twos. Throughout the remainder of the week reinforce the concept by having children work in groups of two, line up in twos, and so on.

Science

● Why Do We Need to Brush?

Materials: one hard-boiled egg with shell, a can of cola, a clear glass, a toothbrush.

Compare the white shell of the egg to children's teeth. *What do you think will happen to the white shell if we place it in this glass of cola?* Have children share predictions and record them on chart paper. Allow the egg to sit in the cola several hours or overnight. Then come together as a group to check predictions. *What happened to the color of the egg? Do you think this is similar to what happens to our teeth when we eat or drink certain foods?* Invite children to revisit why we brush our teeth. Ask them to share what would happen to our teeth if we did not brush them. Remind them that the foods we eat can harm our teeth if we do not brush away the plaque. Using the toothbrush and clean water, brush away the cola from the egg. Children will notice that the stain does not completely disappear. Encourage them to share what we use when we brush to help clean our teeth and keep them strong, healthy, and white (toothpaste).

● Nature's Toothbrush

Materials: Tootsie Roll® candy, baby carrots

Explain to children that we eat smart snacks not only because they are good for our bodies, but because they are also good for our teeth. Have children pair up. Give each child a Tootsie Roll. *Do you think this is a smart snack or a not-so-smart snack? Why?* Have children eat the Tootsie Roll and then look at their partner's teeth. Tell them to open wide and look at what the candy left on their friend's teeth. Now give each child a carrot. *Is this a smart snack or a not-so-smart snack?* Have them eat the carrot and look at their friend's teeth again. *What happened to the candy?* Explain that the carrot "brushed" the candy off the teeth. There are many smart snacks that help to keep our teeth clean in between brushing. Brainstorm smart snacks and record them on chart paper.

Social Studies

Parts of the Mouth

Materials: red posterboard, scissors, pink construction paper, white construction paper, glue, black marker.

Fold the posterboard in half and cut it in the shape of lips. Line the inside with pink construction paper to represent the gums. Use white construction paper to create teeth. Use red construction paper to create a tongue. Label each part. Invite children to come up and point to the parts that you name. Have them explain what each part is used for. The tongue is used for talking, singing, and eating. Teeth are used for biting food, chewing, and smiling. Gums hold our teeth in place and help to keep them strong. The lips are used to form words and keep food inside the mouth.

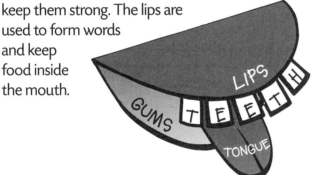

Dental Instruments

Ask your dentist or hygienist to give you some old dental tools. Compare them to the picture of the tools in the Big Book. Invite children to share how each of the tools is used. Pass them around and let them observe how they feel in their hands instead of in their mouth. You might choose to walk around any instruments that have sharp or extremely pointy edges.

Mystery Box

Materials: old shoe box, tape, scissors, dental floss

Tape the lid on an old box and cut a small hole, big enough for a child's hand, in one end. Put a string of dental floss inside the box. Do not let children see you do this. Invite children to sit in a circle and explain that there is something in the box. You are going to pass the box around, and they will reach inside and feel what the object is. They are not to share what they think it is until everyone has had a chance to feel. When the box has gone around the circle ask children yes or no questions. *Is it something you can eat? Can you wear it? Can you play with it? Does it make noise? Can you share it? Is it for your teeth? Do you brush with it? Does it help keep teeth clean and healthy? Can you use it over and over again like a toothbrush? What is it?* Review with children what dental floss is and how it is used. Remind them to have parents help them use dental floss. It should not be something they do on their own.

Visit from a Dentist

Have a dentist or hygienist come to the class to give a presentation on what he or she does during an exam. Prior to the visit, brainstorm with children questions they would like to ask. If you can't find a visitor, send the questions to a dentist and share the results with children. Be sure to have children write thank you notes after the visit or after they receive answers to their questions.

Literature Connection

Bagley, Katie. ***Brush Well: A Look at Dental Care.*** Minnetonka, MN: Bridgestone Books, 2001.

Beeler, Selby. ***Throw Your Tooth on the Roof: Tooth Traditions from Around the World.*** New York, NY: Houghton Mifflin, 1998.

Frost, Helen. ***Food for Healthy Teeth.*** Minnetonka, MN: Pebble Books, 1999.

Grohmann, Almute. ***Dragon Teeth and Parrot Beaks: Even Creatures Brush Their Teeth.*** Carol Stream, IL: Edition Q, 1998.

Jay, Betsy. ***Jane vs. The Tooth Fairy.*** Flagstaff, AZ: Northland Publishing, 2000.

Keller, Laurie. ***Open Wide: Tooth School Inside***. New York, NY: Henry Holt and Company, 2000.

McGinty, Alice. ***Staying Healthy: Dental Care (The Library of Healthy Living).*** New York, NY: Powerkids Press, 1998.

Moss, Miriam. ***Wibble Wobble.*** Wilton, CT: Tiger Tales, 2001.

Munsch, Robert. ***Andrew's Loose Tooth.*** Jefferson City, MO: Cartwheel Books, 1999.

Olson, Mary and Katherine Tillotson. ***Nice Try, Tooth Fairy.*** New York, NY: Simon and Schuster, 2000.

Rowan, Kate. ***I Know Why I Brush My Teeth (Sam's Science).*** Cambridge, PA: Candlewick Press, 1999.

Showers, Paul. ***How Many Teeth? (Let's-Read-and-Find-Out Book).*** New York, NY: HarperCollins, 1991.

Simms, Laura. ***Rotten Teeth.*** New York, NY: Houghton Mifflin Company, 1998.

Stricklin, Julie. ***Those Icky Sticky Smelly Cavity Causing But . . . Invisible Germs.*** St. Paul, MN: Red Leaf Press, 1997.

Wood, Audrey. ***Tooth Fairy.*** England: Childs Play International Limited, 1990.

Assessment Tools

Name: _____ Date: _____

Child's age: _____ Child's Score: ____ /28

Show the child this assessment page and ask: *What are these?*

Child's response: _____

Point to each letter and say: *Tell me what this is.* Record responses in the following ways:

✓ = correct response (Note whether the child identifies the letter by its letter name (L), its letter sound (S), or by a word (W) that begins with that letter.)

✗ = incorrect response

O = no response

Letter Identification (Lowercase)

q ____	f ____	a ____	p ____	e ____
x ____	k ____	n ____	z ____	t ____
i ____	r ____	v ____	j ____	c ____
w ____	g ____	m ____	b ____	h ____
a ____	o ____	u ____	s ____	
l ____	d ____	y ____	g ____	

Assessment Tools

Name: _____   Date: _____

Child's age: _____   Child's Score: _____ /26

Show the child this assessment page and ask: *What are these?*

Child's response: _____

Point to each letter and say: *Tell me what this is.* Record responses in the following ways:

✓ = correct response (Note whether the child identifies the letter by its letter name (L), its letter sound (S), or by a word (W) that begins with that letter.)

✗ = incorrect response

O = no response

Letter Identification (Uppercase)

O____	F____	M____	E____	C____
D____	A____	G____	R____	B____
H____	J____	L____	U____	T____
Y____	S____	P____	X____	K____
N____	I____	Z____		
Q____	W____	V____		

© 2003 Rigby

Assessment Tools

High-Frequency Word and Number Recognition

I	is	the
my	a	and
will	see	1
2	3	4
5	6	7
8	9	10

Assessment Tools

Shape Recognition

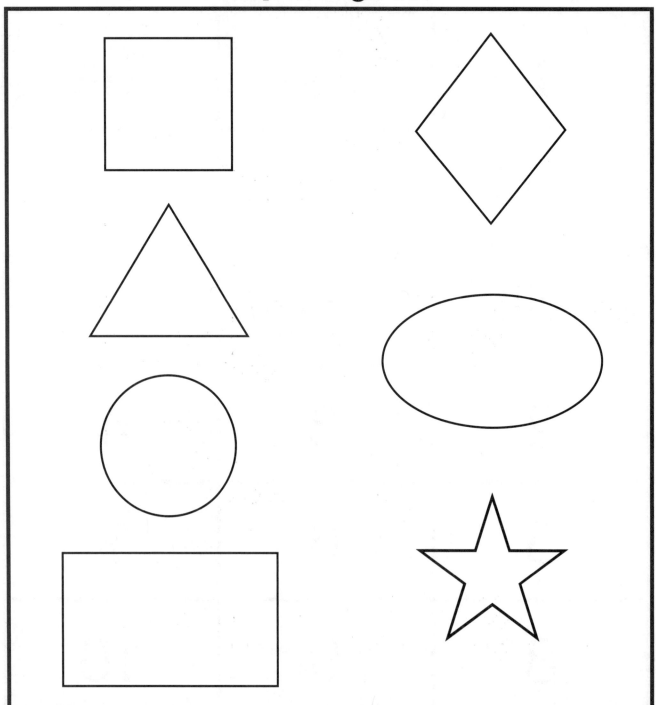

Assessment Tools

Number Correspondence

Directions: Ask the child to color the corresponding number of cubes.

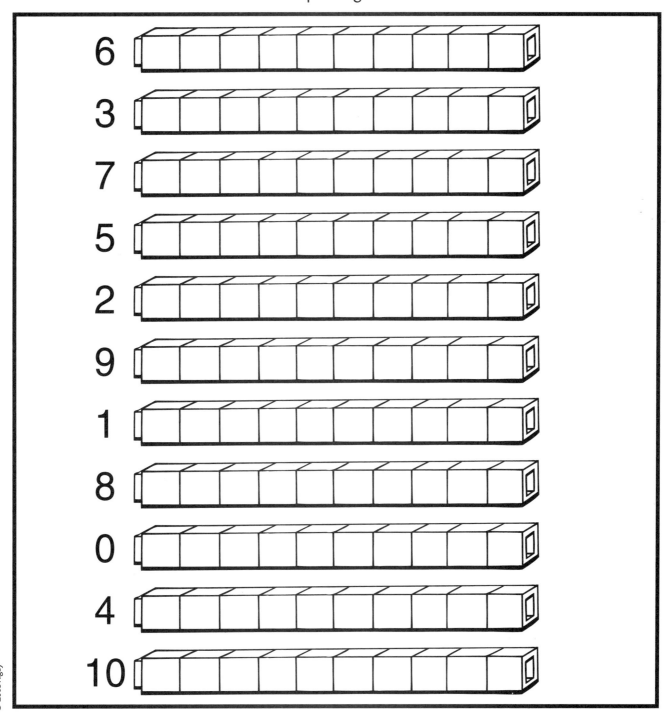

6

3

7

5

2

9

1

8

0

4

10

Assessment Tools

Friends and Me Vocabulary

friendship	share	laugh
care	special	play

Colors and Shapes Vocabulary

circle	square	green
triangle	red	blue

Assessment Tools

Apples Vocabulary

seeds	leaf	core
stem	meat	skin

Harvest Vocabulary

harvest	frost	donation
vine	crop	scarecrow

Assessment Tools

Snow Vocabulary

pair	change	contagious
mittens	gloves	scarf

Polar Animals Vocabulary

hibernate	camouflage	climate
blubber	rookery	snowshoes

Assessment Tools

Nutrition Vocabulary

healthy	diet	protein
pyramid	dairy	dozen

Dental Health Vocabulary

cavity	decay	floss
fluoride	gums	dentist

Concepts About Print Checklist

Name: _____   Date: _____

Concept	Date of Entries								
Identifies the front cover									
Identifies the title									
Demonstrates how to hold a book right-side up in order to read									
Demonstrates how to turn pages									
Demonstrates left-to-right movement									
Demonstrates top-to-bottom movement									
Demonstrates ability to navigate return sweeps (moving from one line of text to the next)									
Demonstrates understanding of a letter									
Demonstrates understanding of a word									
Demonstrates understanding of critical jargon such as first letter, last letter, author, and illustrator									
Demonstrates understanding of one-to-one correspondence									
Demonstrates understanding of picture/text match									